Dig That Site

Dig That Site

Exploring Archaeology, History, and Civilization on the Internet

Gary M. Garfield and Suzanne McDonough

1997
Libraries Unlimited, Inc.
and Its Division
Teacher Ideas Press
Englewood, Colorado

LIBRARIES UNLIMITED, INC.
and Its Division
Teacher Ideas Press
P.O. Box 6633
Englewood, CO 80155-6633
1-800-237-6124
www.lu.com

Constance Hardesty
Project Editor

Sheryl Tongue
Design and Composition

Images copyright
New Vision Technologies Inc.

Library of Congress Cataloging-in-Publication Data

Garfield, Gary M.
    Dig that site : exploring archaeology, history, and civilization on the Internet /
Gary M. Garfield and Suzanne McDonough.
        ix, 135 p. 22×28 cm.
        Includes bibliographical references (p. 125) and index.
        ISBN 1-56308-534-8
        1. Archaeology—Computer network resources.   2. Civilization, ancient--Computer
network resources.   3. Internet (Computer network)
I. McDonough, Suzanne, 1959–   .   II. Title.
CC82.9.G37   1997
    930.1'028'5--dc-21   97-11167
                                                                              CIP

Contents

Africa 55

North America 69

South America 91

Figures

Introduction

Dig That Site: Exploring Archaeology, History, and Civilization on the Internet combines the excitement of the Internet with conventional learning resources to explore early civilizations and cultures. Combining the fascination of archaeology and the Internet with hands-on classroom activities, *Dig That Site* encourages independent student research, problem solving, and decision making. This book takes teachers and elementary school students on a journey that exemplifies a new way of thinking, teaching, and learning. The national movement in education for students to seek "infinite" resources through various media, including electronic media, unquestionably supports these objectives.

Dig That Site is for every teacher who wants to explore ancient and historical civilizations, peoples, regions, origins, and ancestors. *Dig That Site* not only prepares students for the journey but guides them to special archaeological sites. Ideas, procedures, and the use of the Internet in the classroom are discussed in terms that can be easily understood by the novice as well as the more advanced computer user. *Dig That Site* provides meaningful integration of this powerful technology within the standard school curriculum, enabling teachers to provide rich, enlightening, and engaging learning experiences for all learners.

About the Sites in This Book

The authors have selected and previewed Internet resources related to archaeological sites on all seven continents. Internet resources are of immediate use and interest to students as they dig into the ancient and historical puzzles of our world. Archaeology and cultures are explored in a way that is memorable because students visit the various sites via the Internet. Students navigate the Internet, traveling from Italy's Pompeii to France's ancient painted caves, from Mayan ruins in Honduras to the temples of the Middle East. (For ease of use, we use current, rather than historical, names to indicate the location of each site. It is important to remember, however, that political boundaries and country names change over time.) Students learn the geography, history, art, and culture of the civilization being explored. The sites are listed by continent. The complete Internet address is given for each site. Also, each site is accompanied by practical, hands-on classroom lessons that integrate various subjects across the curriculum. In addition, many of the sites are linked to related Internet sites for further exploration. This linking demonstrates the power of the Internet as an educational vehicle. As new and varied sites become available, you and your students will quickly become independent site experts.

Our goal is to help you become more comfortable with this technology and to help you use it, in combination with other library resources, in the discovery of the past. This enables students to participate in rich, relevant, motivational discovery. In our technological global community, it is more and more apparent that students and teachers are exploring and learning side by side. Teachers are able to plan and implement instruction using new tools, materials, and delivery systems. They can help students engage in a fascinating study that previously was driven by limited resources. The teacher assumes the role of resource person or, perhaps, an important conduit to discovery as students of all ages search, inquire, discuss, solve problems, and make important learning decisions. Students are no longer passive learners of history but become archaeologists, searching, constructing, making assumptions, and drawing conclusions related to their findings. The teacher is a facilitator of inquiry, assisting with the process, aiding in the challenge, and watching and guiding as students begin to ask powerful questions. Both teacher and student embark on teaching–learning endeavors that are a departure from previous experience.

Welcome to the Dig

Welcome to the world of the archaeologist, the scientist whose work links us with the past. You might first ask, What is an archaeologist? Is it the character who digs up artifacts or partakes in the wild-world adventures of Indiana Jones? Or is the archaeologist a thorough academician who works both in the lab and in the field to answer the untold questions of the world's past? The answer is: both. The archaeologist searches for clues and artifacts that aid in the reconstruction of the puzzles of the past. At each Internet site, students will experience the knowledge gained from the often-painstaking efforts of these professional women and men.

To dig is to search, whether with a bulldozer, shovel, small dust brush, or microscope. Also, a dig is a site where the archaeological team believes the clues of the past are waiting to be unveiled. A dig may be found in the heart of a modern, cosmopolitan city; in the jungles of the rain forest; or on the ocean floor. It doesn't matter to the archaeologist where a dig is located, only that it is there waiting to be visited.

The Internet: A Bridge to the Past

In our study of archaeology, whether it takes us to the fortresses of the ancient Chinese or the homes of the Pueblo Native Americans, we look at history using the tools of tomorrow; this unique approach provides a unique mix of the past, present, and future. We soon alter the way we construct ideas and images of history. The book becomes only one of the many resources we seek, as we now possess worldwide contributions, literally at our fingertips. As students delve into the archives assembled by social scientists, they have the opportunity to write their own personal commentaries about cultures and events.

The Internet is becoming the world's richest depository for archaeological information and study. Through the digital archives of the Internet, the great scholars and archaeologists of the twentieth century are assembling accessible, scientific, user-friendly information. At no other time in our history have we had the opportunity to study the past so easily. Access from home, library, or school permits us to travel in time for myriad historical experiences, enriching our knowledge base and enhancing our lives.

With Wisdom We Question

With digital media, as with print, film, and video, it is all too easy to accept the formal presentation of any subject as the truth. We hear quotations and citations from various books or journals, from a television program or from the newspaper. More than ever, because of the increasing access to the Internet, both in retrieval and deposit, we must be willing to verify facts and seek credibility in sources. Most moderately computer-literate individuals are capable of developing a home page that, by its polished presentation, offers persuasive evidence that what is written must be important, if not true. Teachers and students should be open to new information, yet questioning. Look to the source and learn to be prudent consumers of this information that belongs to us all.

Preparing for the Dig

Before you begin to use the tools for this unique study, we strongly recommend you offer your students a brief introduction to archaeology. Most of us, when we're starting out, don't know much about archaeology. No problem. With a few basic books, a videotape or two, and a visit to the school library media specialist, your knowledge will increase tenfold. And, remember, you'll be learning along with your students. In your new role, you are not dispensing information, but rather facilitating or managing resources so that your students (and you) become self-initiating learners. You should, however, understand the basic tools of the study so that you can effectively direct students to use them wisely. The following ideas and activities may facilitate this exciting journey.

A Basic Concept: The Trash Can

The trash receptacle is an essential tool for introducing the concept of archaeology. (See pages 14–15 for a trash can activity.) The simple classroom trash container records, in order, most events that occur each day. Thus, the classroom culture is archived in nice, neat layers, as might be the culture of an ancient civilization. In the context of archaeology, trash and trash containers take on a whole new and important meaning.

The School Dig Site

Constructing your own dig site at the school is a great way to practice using some of the introductory conceptual and physical tools of archaeologists. You may not want to bring out the jackhammers or bulldozers, but you can certainly show students your site and let them know that they will be discovering the mysteries that lay within. (See pages 13–14 for details about how to carry out this activity.)

A Good Costume

As you research and read, start putting together your archaeologist costume so that you can enact the character as you teach. This is an easy task. You will discover many options for your costume, depending on the period and the type of exploration you are engaged in. Some basics are boots, blue jeans, tool belt, work shirt, hat, and a variety of brushes and picks to hang from your tool belt. If you want to lean to the British, think about puffed cuff trousers, suspenders, and a walking stick. For cave explorers, known as spelunkers, a hard hat and helmet light are essentials. Visit the library for ideas, or look for authentic apparel on the Internet sites.

A Few Heavy Tools for Authenticity

To heighten the sense of authenticity and enhance the classroom climate, assemble and display a variety of tools, such as shovels, picks, rakes, brushes, screens, a hose, wheelbarrow, flashlight, and anything else you think might be needed on a dig. The students can add to the toolshed as they learn more.

Record the Events for All to See

Every good archaeologist needs a place to display the current project, and that is why you construct your wonderful archaeological classroom bulletin board. You might want to include some general information about archaeology as well as exciting facts related to the current dig. Get out your camera to capture the adventure, and post your pictures for all to see. This will be a tremendous display to share with parents and visitors during open house.

Your bulletin board may also incorporate a minimuseum that displays the many artifacts from the site.

Don't forget the day-to-day records. Make sure students have an adequate supply of paper and pencils (or printers and ribbons) to record information from both Internet sites and more conventional sources. A personal journal is included as appendix A for you and your students to use in taking notes about new sites they discover as they explore the Internet.

Information Tools: Books, Periodicals, CD-ROMs, and Videos

Augment Internet resources with more conventional sources, such as books, magazines, CD-ROMs, videotapes, audio tapes, and laser disks. Your school or district media specialist can recommend materials appropriate for your study. The library media specialist may be able to help you select appropriate materials or ideas for curricular integration. Also look for other resources related to the topic of archaeology or to the specific site you will be exploring. These might be part of a larger display or part of a research resource library you and the students create in a corner of the classroom.

Essential Tools for Telecommunications

The essential tools for excavating the online site are the computer, modem, and phone line or cable. This book assumes you have some basic knowledge and experience with telecommunications. Here again, you may wish to ask your school library media specialist or technology mentor teacher for assistance. Also, you may want to secure one of the telecommunications resource books for teachers or call one of the resources listed in appendix B.

Surprises for Field Workers

Remember, your students are no longer schoolchildren, they are explorers of ancient and historical civilizations. Going into the field always involves a few surprises, so bring along some interesting children's books that are related to the site or culture you are exploring. Don't forget a few bags of snacks for all to enjoy!

Organization in the Classroom

What should the room look like? Which kids use the computer and when? The answer is simple. Do what is comfortable for you. Try to find a system that fits your style and basic philosophy of teaching. Design your room in any way that best fits the layout of the room, furnishings, number of students, and your teaching style (see figure 1). We suggest students work in cooperative groups and participate together in projects, engaging in research, going online, and forming conclusions together. Figure 1 offers some suggestions for those of you who have computers in your classroom. There is no one correct way to organize your classroom; your well-thought-through method will be the best. Simply remember that you are doing something new, allowing for new ways of teaching and new ways of learning. Be flexible, provide excitement in the delivery of instruction, and try to maximize all aspects of this very special event.

Planning, Procedures, and Assessment

Give me my daily planner, grade book, and an electronic calendar! You will need to organize the study so that it holds meaning for you and the learners. Think about introducing the study of archaeology to your class in new and different ways so students see the practical applications as

Maps, Screen, and White Board

Classroom Traditional
Resource Center

Mounted
Television Monitor

Video Player

Overhead
Projector

Door

Student Desks

Teacher's Center

Computer Stations with Modem/Internet Connection
Television Monitor Viewing Capability

Printer

Software, Digital Camera, CD-ROMs,
Video Tapes, Scanners, Miscellaneous Cables

Door

Figure 1.   A sample configuration for computers in the classroom.

well as the connections to our lives. Decide how you are going to group your students and how many times per week you will be archaeologists. Determine when your groups will do library research, online searching, and other data collection. Plan full-class activities so they complement the current subject of study. Lay out your procedures and safety rules, and be sure your students understand your expectations. Organize your assessment instruments and procedures, whether they are based on observation, process, or product. Plan bulletin boards, acquisition of materials, and documentation. Discuss the possibilities with your colleagues. Think about participating in this study within a grade-level team.

If you want a little more support, e-mail the authors. You can reach us at:

gmgarfield@csupomona.edu   or   smcdono@cyberg8t.com

Accessing the Sites

To access a site, you and your adventurers will need to find a guide to lead the way. To use the Internet, you will need a provider. Many teachers and schools subscribe to an online commercial service, such as Prodigy, America Online, CompuServe, etc. These services allow access to the Internet. This is an easy-to-use, convenient way to explore the Internet. In addition to the online commercial service, you or your school are probably subscribing to a private or county-contracted Internet access provider, which for a flat fee can give you almost unlimited access to the wonders of the Internet. When you sign up, the service provider will give you, at no additional charge, the software you need to navigate the Internet. Typically, teachers get a hefty discount from Internet service providers. You should be able to get local access at 150 hours per month for about $15 per month. (Don't forget to ask for the teacher's discount. If your service provider won't give you a teacher's discount, move along until you find one that will.) More and more providers are opening every week, so check in your local newspaper (often in the sports or business sections) or consult the business pages of the telephone book. If you have trouble finding a provider, call a local computer store or university computer department and ask for advice.

What You Will Discover on the Internet

The Internet will allow you to navigate to faraway places simply and quickly. For our purposes, you will find an almost endless and constantly growing array of new and interesting archaeological sites containing information for you and your students to explore and study. You'll find photographs, drawings, stories, charts, and more information than you can imagine. Yet, one of the most exciting things about exploring sites on the Internet is the infinite possibilities of site links related to the topic of study. As you explore both the Internet and traditional resources, you'll discover new sites.

The Integrated Curriculum

Telecommunications must be integrated into the curriculum and never be used as a stand-alone activity. *Dig That Site* offers an integrated thematic curriculum that engages students in the fascinating study of archaeology, history, and culture, yet extends through geography, art, science, music, movement, language arts, and mathematics. Figure 2 shows how this integrated curriculum can be achieved. Figure 3 is a tracking chart for a classroom with students involved in multiple technology applications across the integrated curriculum.

Theme: Ancient Egypt

Literature   *The Egypt Game* by Zilpha Keatley Snyder

This Newbery Honor book tells the story of two young girls who share a love for ancient Egypt. Together they create and enjoy a new game, until strange things begin to happen. Join the adventure!

Technology Applications:
- Using e-mail, contact a classroom in another part of the state or country and share an online book talk. As each class reads the novel, discuss online the theme, setting, characters, and plot.
- Using an Internet search engine, seek information about the author.

Language Arts   Hieroglyphics

Using ancient Egyptian hieroglyphics, students will create stories about early life in Egypt.

Technology Applications:
- Contact experts in the field of Egyptology via e-mail addresses found on the Internet. Begin a dialogue by contacting the University of Cairo. Ask the scholars to provide insight and opinions about the hieroglyphics that students have collected.
- Using a drawing program (e.g., KidsPix), instruct students to create colorful hieroglyphic symbols. These can be presented as a slide show within the program, or they can be printed on a color printer, laminated, and posted in the classroom.

Social Studies   Interactive Simulation using *Mummy's Message*

Students will participate in an interactive simulation related to an archaeological expedition into a pyramid. In cooperative groups, students will make choices and decisions as they learn about the problems and successes of the site excavation. Contact Interact Company, Box 262, Lakeside, CA 92040 for more information about the simulation program *Mummy's Message*.

Technology Applications:
- Have students use a word processing program to keep a classroom journal as they imagine what it would be like to be archaeologists. Each day one student documents what the class has learned about Egypt.
- Students explore the music of ancient Egypt by researching the musical instruments of the ancient culture. Students can create their own instruments based on their research. Contact local music stores for CDs that showcase the music or instruments of ancient Egypt.

Science   Medicine of Ancient Egypt

Students will discover the highly advanced medical practices of the ancient Egyptians.

Technology Applications:
- Contact district, county, and private video archives for titles appropriate to the study of ancient Egypt. These are usually available to teachers for short periods of time, from three days to one week.

Continued on next page

Figure 2.   Integrated curriculum unit about Egypt.

Theme: Ancient Egypt

- Instruct students to research specific topics using multimedia CD-ROMs, CD-ROM encyclopedias, and Internet Web sites. Students can use the collected information to create their own multimedia presentations.

Math   Pyramids

Students will learn about geometry as related to the pyramid form and participate in activities to study this shape.

Technology Applications:
- Discover ancient Egypt and the pyramids using the interactive CD-ROM *Imagination Express: Destination Pyramids* by Edmark. Students can create interactive stories as they explore the pyramids using this theme-focused learning program.
- Visit and explore the pyramids of Egypt on the Internet. Instruct students about the use of search engines for collecting information on specific topics related to the mathematical applications seen in the pyramids. Bookmark these sites for later use in classroom projects, multimedia presentations, or traditional research reports. Some good Web sites are:

http://pharos.bu.edu/Egypt/Wonders/pyramid.html

http://galaxy.cau.edu/tsmith/Gpyr.html

http://199.182.229.110/Exhibits/ADAE/fig23d.htm

http://pami.uwaterloo.ca/~reda/kings/kings.html

http://www1.usa1.com/~madartis/EGYPT/EGYPT.html

http://www1.usa1.com/~madartis/EGYPT/alphabet.html

Culmination   Archaeological Dig

Students will participate in a simulated archaeological dig to uncover buried objects that are representative of those discovered in Egypt.

Technology Application:
- Document the culmination archaeological dig using a digital camera or 35-mm camera. Include all phases of the excavation. Instruct students to create a Web site to document their activity. As a safety precaution, avoid posting photographs of students on the Web site. However, do include images of the artifacts, as well as researched information and links to related sites.

Figure 2.   Integrated curriculum unit about Egypt (continued).

Classroom Computer Schedule

✔ Indicates student has completed assigned task.

Student	Computer One	Computer Two	Computer Three
	Thematic CD-ROM Edmark: Pyramids	Internet Access Net Search URLs	Word Processing ClarisWorks
Gilbert	✔	✔	
Jessica		✔	✔
Rand	✔	✔	✔
Cory		✔	✔
Shantell	✔		✔
Jennifer	✔	✔	✔
Joey	✔	✔	
Charlotte	✔		✔
Rodrigo	✔	✔	✔
Jackie	✔	✔	✔
Ana	✔	✔	
Suzanne	✔	✔	
Carolyn		✔	✔
Marissa	✔		✔
Billy	✔	✔	✔
Ian	✔	✔	✔
Bob	✔		✔

Figure 3.   Classroom computer schedule for three applications that reinforce the integrated thematic unit.

Diversity and Cooperative Learning

Working together in our classroom community is certainly as important as, or more important than, the product. Brainstorming, planning, designing, assuming tasks, sharing ideas, and collecting and analyzing data are critical activities for students to engage in when attempting to meet objectives. Cooperative grouping is the social pattern in school, play, and work. By the nature of our diverse classrooms and the diversity of our curriculum, the study of archaeology and ancient civilizations promotes understanding of peoples now and throughout history. We study and learn with students of many cultures, and we study and learn about many cultures. As a community, we explore our lives and the lives of people who preceded us as we understand and connect the many links in the long chain of culture and civilization.

The Library As Source

The library plays a pivotal role in our exploration. Until most recently, much of the research data and conclusions related to archaeology and ancient civilizations were accessible through libraries around the world. The library has been evolving for centuries, from private collections, independent research centers, private archives, government ware-houses, foundations, educational institutions, and public depositories. Since the early 1970s, libraries have been working to make their collections widely available through computer networks. Expanding their holdings in physical media and extending their reach online, libraries serve all those who have a need or interest.

Finding Your Way to the Sites

As inquiring student archaeologists, we continually seek our sites in the most expedient fashion. Choose the search methods that are consistent with the abilities of your learners, the level of interest, and the complexity of the task. The following four approaches will move you and your young archaeological apprentices to the amazing sites as quickly as possible.

Search by Continent

Using the table of contents, you and your team can identify sites by continent. Use this method to complement the study of a culture or region or to explore related themes in literature, history, or social studies. On each continent, students will become acquainted with authentic archaeological sites. For each site is given a location marker referenced on the world map, a timeline offering perspectives related to historical events, and a brief description of the site. Also given, of course, is the Internet address, or URL, for the Internet site corresponding to the archaeological site. Our young explorers simply copy the URL into the Locator box and hit Return (or Enter); in seconds they will be deep in the dig.

Search Alphabetically

If you know the name or location of an archaeological site, students can use the site index at the back of this book to find it. The index provides the page number on which the URL is found. Again, students simply copy the URL to the Locator box and hit Return (or Enter) to quickly travel to their chosen site.

Conventional Libraries to Cyberspace

Archaeology inquiry may involve traditional, hands-on library work. Perhaps you are seeking Internet resources about an archaeological site, but you are not certain of its locale or name. Searching materials in the library by subject or related topics, you may find key words you can then use to search the Internet. (For tips on searching the Internet, see the following section.)

You will probably find valuable resources in various libraries as well as on the Internet. The Internet is young, and the information on it does not yet rival the resources available from institutional libraries. As mentioned earlier, libraries and the Internet both provide resources useful for research. Like archaeologists, we use all the resources at our disposal to solve the mysteries of ancient and historical civilizations.

Using Search Engines

The term *search engine* may conjure the whirling wheels, spinning gears, and exploding speed of a vehicle that will take you on your travels. Internet search engines can quickly take you where you want to go. Using key words you supply, search engines quickly search thousands of pieces of information and provide an index to related sites. As with any vehicle, it is less important that you know how it works than that you know how to use it. To search the Internet, simply select one of a dozen popular search engines. Some well-known search engines are Alta Vista, Infoseek, Magellan, Lycos, and Yahoo. Most users develop a preference for one or another based on speed, screen layout, indexing features, readability, or habit. Generally, to use a search engine, you click on a button that is marked "Net Search." This button usually appears on your graphic browser when you start an Internet session. When you click on this button, a list of various search engines appears. Click on one. The search engine will open. Instructions for searching will appear on the screen. Usually, you will be asked to type key words for your search; within seconds, a list of Internet sites related to your key words appears. If you type *archaeology France*, for example, a list of Internet sites related to these descriptors appears. (The lists can be quite long, because most search engines will include in the list any site that contains both words. Be careful to choose specific key words—and to spell them correctly—to get the best results.) Scroll down the list to find a useful site, and click on that item. The home page of the selected site appears. After you have studied the site, you can either follow a link to a related Web page or return to the index to make another selection. At any time, you can either print out your Internet finds or copy them to disk for future use.

Use Some Caution When in the Field

Parents, school leaders, or others may seek your opinion about the selection and viewing of material available on the Internet. It may not be necessary to engage school proctors to guard the monitor, but with good sense, clearly established parameters, appropriate positioning of the computer, proper supervision, and a climate of trust, few issues of propriety should arise. Recent Supreme Court decisions have protected the Internet from government censorship. It is the classroom teacher's responsibility to implement and maintain appropriate access to material. State the standards in very clear terms and be sure they are accepted by every student. This will result in a positive and productive classroom community.

Exploration Begins Here

Patience is the order of the day for archaeological adventurers in the field. Give your students plenty of time to explore the many archaeology sites on the seven continents. With each exploration comes excitement, new knowledge, and a view of our past.

Where Will We Go?

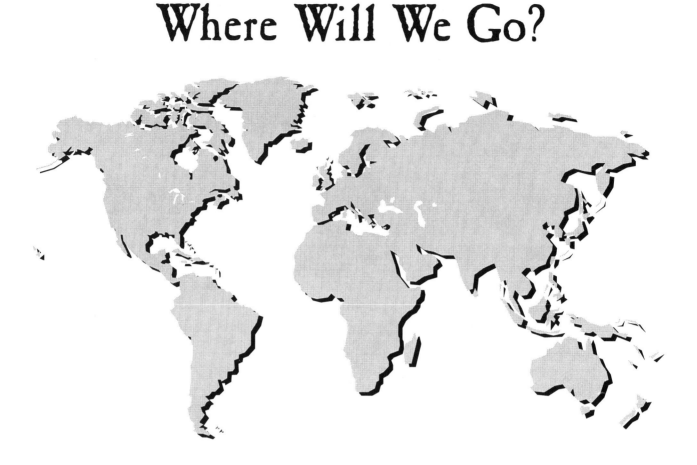

Africa
The Pyramids of Giza, Egypt
The Great Enclosure, Zimbabwe
Tomb of Tutankhamen, Egypt
Ancient Port of Carthage, Tunisia

Antarctica
The History Site
The Davis and Mawson Stations
The Discovery Hut
Expedition Map of Antarctica

Asia
Beirut, Lebanon
Masada, Israel
The Dead Sea Scrolls, Israel
Tomb of Qin Shihuangdi, China
Marki Alonia, Cyprus
Petra, Jordan

Australia and the Pacific
Shipwrecks of Queensland, Australia
Aboriginal Stone Tools
Easter Island

Europe
Athens, Greece
Pompeii, Italy
Paleolithic-Era Painted Caves, France
Stonehenge, England
Vikings and Norsemen, Scandinavia

North America
Jackson's Hermitage, United States
The Anasazi, Mesa Verde, United States
Jamestown, Virginia, United States
The Maya, Mexico and Central America
The Aztecs, Mexico
The Thule, Arctic North America

South America
Tiwanaku, Bolivia
Caverna da Pedra Pintada, Brazil
Machu Picchu, Peru
Nazcan Lines, Peru

Don't Put On Your Boots Yet

Lesson One: The Great Archaeological Dig

Objective

Students will participate in an archaeological dig to uncover buried objects that represent artifacts. Students will collect discovered fragment artifacts, reconstruct them, and make conclusions related to their origins.

Time Required

One hour

Materials

- ☐ Designated digging site (This might be an area partitioned off in a playground area, a large sandbox, or a plastic bucket filled with dirt.)
- ☐ Digging tools, for example, hand shovels, spoons, tongue depressors, little fingers and hands
- ☐ Small, clean paintbrushes and toothbrushes for removing soil
- ☐ Fragment artifacts that can be buried
- ☐ Large site: string, marking sticks, broken ceramic vases and/or pots, sculptured clay figures, large beef bones, ceramic glue
- ☐ Small site: buckets or shoe boxes, plastic or glass beads (approximately six per student), leather lacing

Procedure

Depending on your school environment and the willingness of your administration, you can do the archaeological dig one of two ways. If you can obtain permission to dig up the playground or the seldom-used rose garden outside the principal's office, the site can be established outdoors.

Prior to the arrival of students, randomly bury an assortment of artifacts within the designated area. It is also recommended that the area be sectioned off with bright orange cones and signs "DANGER: ARCHAEOLOGICAL SITE," to keep students who are not involved in the activity away from the area. Section and mark off the area to be used with string and stakes. Divide the parcel of ground into four to six sections so that cooperative student groups can be responsible for a given section of the dig site.

Instruct the class how they should work as an excavation team and emphasize the importance of being careful not to damage any of the items uncovered. Allow the students free exploration when "digging that site."

Provide an area, such as a large table or roped-off area near a building, to place the fragments as the children begin to make their many discoveries. After the fragments are collected, have the children reassemble and glue together the pieces. When completed, the reconstructed artifacts can be displayed in your school or classroom museum. Use a shelf in the library, a lighted display cabinet in the school hallway, or a countertop in your classroom.

If you need to confine the dig to the classroom, bury the artifacts in six to eight shoe boxes or plastic buckets filled with dirt. Plastic beads work especially well in these smaller excavation sites. Each box or bucket should contain enough beads so that individual students can string the beads on a leather lace and wear as a bracelet. Place the boxes on paper-covered tables. In cooperative working groups, begin the excavation. Be sure to remind the students to keep as much of the dig as possible on the tabletop. The night custodian may not see the historical value of this dirt.

Lesson Two: The Trash Can

What has greater similarity to an authentic archaeological dig than a trash receptacle? In fact, many of the world's famous digs that aid in the reconstruction of ancient cultures are, in fact, refuse centers of that culture. Thus, the classroom trash receptacle is an essential tool for introducing the concept of archaeology. There, the classroom "culture" like the culture of ancient civilizations, is archived in nice neat layers. Trash and trash containers take on a whole new and important meaning.

Objective

Students will reconstruct the class activities by using the class trash receptacle as a layered archaeological site.

Time Required

One hour

Materials

☐ Rubber surgical gloves
☐ Wooden tongs
☐ Paper
☐ Pencils

Procedure

First, the teacher should save the tall classroom trash bin or several smaller ones for an entire day. You might notify the students to dispose of tissues in another closed container provided. Discuss with the students the procedures for examining an archaeological site:

1. Move slowly down through the layers.
2. Catalog each artifact recovered.
3. Attempt to make assumptions about the use or purpose of the artifact.
4. Maintain the order recovered for each artifact.
5. Attempt to develop a timeline as to when the artifact was used. In this case, whether the artifact was used in the early or late morning, afternoon, and so on.
6. What assumptions can be made about the culture based solely on the artifact recovered?

With the class divided into cooperative archaeological teams, distribute the rubber gloves, tongs, paper, and pencils. Instruct the students on their roles as archaeologists. Check their understanding of the steps for the site process. Emphasize the need for care and caution. Let the dig begin!

At the conclusion, have the students display their artifact list and the conclusions they have made. Discuss both the displayed products and the process. Now your group is ready to accompany Indiana Jones.

Lesson Three: So You Want to Be an Archaeologist?

Objective

Students will do research to determine the requirements for a career as a professional or amateur archaeologist.

Time Required

One hour

Materials

- ☐ Writing materials
- ☐ Internet resources
- ☐ Library resources

Procedure

Review with the students the objective of the lesson. This project is very open and encourages independence, offering students choices as to which resources they will utilize to accumulate data.

Let the students approach this as an inquiry lesson, utilizing the teacher as a resource person. Allow the students to brainstorm in groups or as individuals, whatever they choose. Allow them to decide whom they will contact to secure the data. Encourage students or direct them in this process. *Do not provide them with the resources.* However, you might suggest the following:

1. Students might find an interesting archaeological Home Page on the Internet and can e-mail the author. Before this is done, the teacher MUST approve the site and the correspondent. The student can interview the archaeologist, discovering various aspects of the job and professional preparation. This approach has some wonderful possibilities.

2. Contact a university or college department of archaeology on the Internet and begin an interview correspondence with a faculty member. Again, all correspondence must have teacher approval.

3. Students can send "snail mail" letters to archaeologists. Names of prominent archaeologists can be secured through book publishers, newspapers, and research publications.

4. Use the classroom phone to make phone calls to archaeologists. These should be relatively local, or the district budget manager will come digging for you. Attempt to find information on becoming an archaeologist or locate sites with activities for amateurs.

5. Contact university, college, or high school career centers related to this field. Personnel at these departments should be able to assist in obtaining additional information.

When students feel satisfied with the data collection, they can assemble a report of their findings. Students can share the results of the inquiry process.

Lesson Four: Ethics and Archaeology

From what we have observed, legitimate archaeologists often must disturb the evidence of the past in order to reach conclusions. For most scientists, ethical practices prevail as to how they accomplish their work.

Objective

Students will discuss the ethical considerations of exploring archaeological sites when that work has an impact on descendants of that civilization.

Time Required

Thirty minutes

Materials

☐ Paper
☐ Pencil

Procedures

The teacher will conduct a sensitive discussion of the ethics of archaeological exploration when it affects living people or animals. The teacher may wish to discuss the issues through an inquiry process, having students write ideas (individually or in groups) and participate in class dialogue. Sensitivity and respect should always prevail. The following questions may be raised in this discussion:

Should archaeologists explore the sacred burial grounds of indigenous peoples? Why? Why not? What are the alternatives? What are the rights and sensitivities of the descendants?

Should scientists raise the famous passenger ship the *Titanic*, which serves as a grave for over a thousand people? Why? Why not? How do the students think the relatives of the deceased passengers feel about these activities?

Can your students think of other ethical situations that raise questions for the work of archaeologists?

Following the group or individual reports, students should share their conclusions. Because of the sensitive nature of this topic, a feedback session should also be conducted.

Asia

Beirut, Lebanon

Masada, Israel

The Dead Sea Scrolls, Israel

Tomb of Qin Shihuangdi, China

Marki Alonia, Cyprus

Petra, Jordan

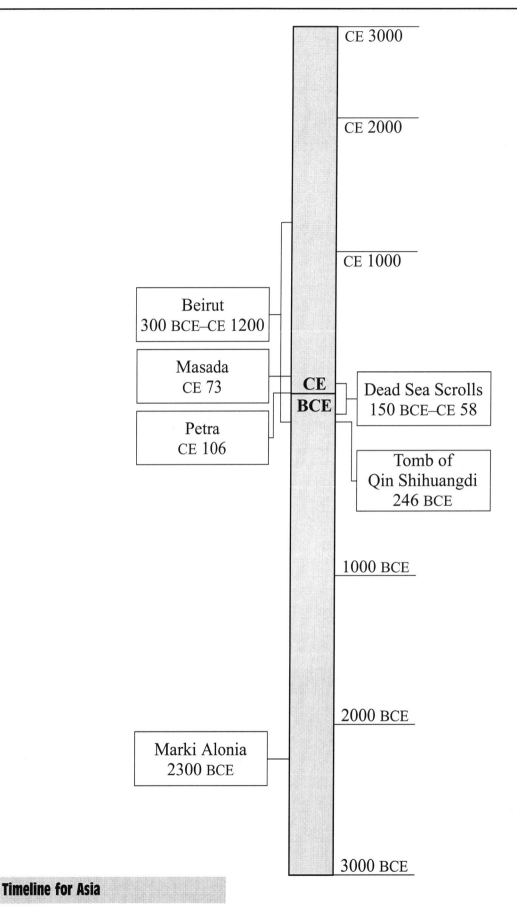

CE 3000

CE 2000

CE 1000

Beirut
300 BCE–CE 1200

Masada
CE 73

CE
BCE

Dead Sea Scrolls
150 BCE–CE 58

Petra
CE 106

Tomb of
Qin Shihuangdi
246 BCE

1000 BCE

2000 BCE

Marki Alonia
2300 BCE

3000 BCE

Timeline for Asia

Asia

The continent of Asia is probably the most diverse of all the seven continents. It is the largest in total area and population with a third of the world's land and over a fifth of its population. The highest and lowest spots on the earth are located in Asia. The continent extends from Europe and Africa on the west to the Pacific Ocean in the east. It reaches the frigid Arctic on the north and extends south to the tropics. During your visit, you will discover both the ancient and modern characteristics of this wondrous continent. Travel from ancient markets, or souks, to the modern ones, where it appears that time has stood still, or from ancient lands of yesterday to some of the most modern cities on earth.

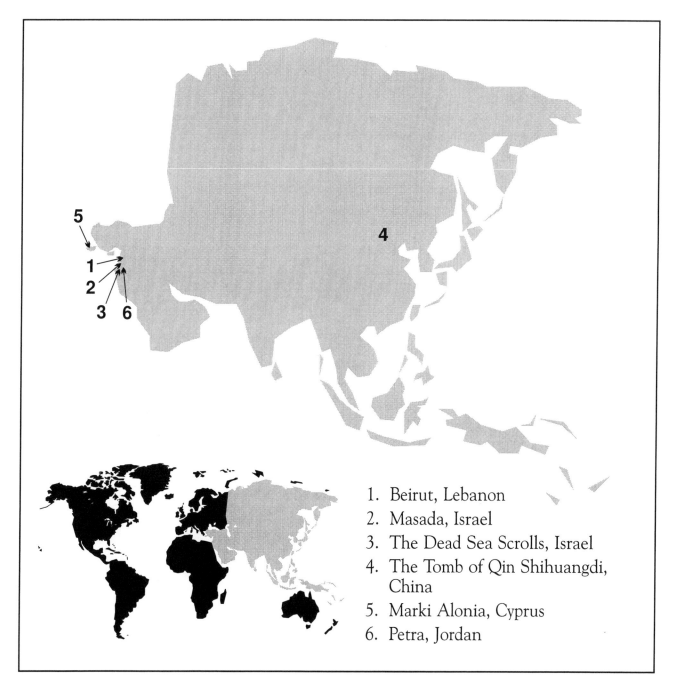

1. Beirut, Lebanon
2. Masada, Israel
3. The Dead Sea Scrolls, Israel
4. The Tomb of Qin Shihuangdi, China
5. Marki Alonia, Cyprus
6. Petra, Jordan

Beirut, Lebanon

http://www.hiof.no/aub/aub-online/faculties/arts_and_sciences/archaeology/index.html

Located on the eastern Mediterranean Sea, Beirut has had a rich history. Once known as the Jewel of the Mediterranean, this site can be used as a timeline for studying the many peoples that have called this country home. The Phoenicians founded Beirut in about 3000 BCE. A succession of foreign rulers controlled the area throughout most of its history. They include the Assyrians, Greeks, Romans, Ottoman Turks, and French. Even in this decade, the city of Beirut has been embroiled in a tragic civil war.

On the Web site, enter the ancient souks (markets) of downtown Beirut as archaeologists begin the study of the war-torn area that is providing scientists with a view of life in the Middle East over a several-thousand-year period. Archaeologists anticipate finding literally millions of shards and other artifacts deposited from the third century BCE through the twelfth century CE and beyond. View pictures of the Islamic, Hellenistic, Roman, Byzantine, Medieval and modern eras. This site is like a ladder for the explorer that extends down through thousands of years.

Lesson One: A Taste of the Ancient Market

Objective

Students will prepare a midafternoon snack reminiscent of the food served by merchants in the Middle Eastern souk.

Time Required

Thirty minutes

Materials

- ☐ Mixing bowls
- ☐ Mortar and pestle (or small blender)
- ☐ Strainer or colander
- ☐ Knife
- ☐ Mixing and serving spoons
- ☐ Four cans of chick peas (garbanzo beans)
- ☐ Five cloves of garlic
- ☐ ½ cup olive oil
- ☐ Two lemons or lemon juice
- ☐ Water
- ☐ Salt and pepper
- ☐ Pita bread (½ pocket per student)
- ☐ Sliced or chopped olives

☐ Feta or jack cheese

☐ Tomatoes (optional)

☐ Anything else you think the children would like to put in the sandwich

Procedures

Walk down the back streets of the ancient or modern souk and you will encounter aromas of spices and oils that have awakened the senses of travelers for thousands of years. In this activity your young archaeologists will have the opportunity to prepare a traditional Middle Eastern meal that is sure to please.

1. Post the recipe as you review procedures with students in one of the interest groups.

2. Drain and rinse the garbanzo beans.

3. Have students mash the beans to a thick paste using the mortar and pestle or small blender.

4. Do the same to the garlic (discard any garlic pieces).

5. Add enough oil to make the paste smooth. Add a couple teaspoons of lemon juice and a few drops of water to thin the paste. Remember, few ancient people had an exact recipe, so work with it until you think you have it right. It should have the consistency of a thin paste or dip.

6. Add just a tiny pinch of salt and pepper.

7. Grate the jack cheese or break apart the feta cheese.

8. Open the can of olives, drain, and set aside.

9. Holding open the half pita pocket, spoon in a little hummus, add some of the sliced olives, sprinkle in some cheese, and you are there! Enjoy.

Lesson Two: Pottery of Beirut

Objective

The students will paint terra-cotta pots with designs found on the artifacts of ancient Beirut.

Time Required

Forty-five minutes

Materials

☐ Terra-cotta pots of different sizes and shapes

☐ Black tempera paint

☐ Paintbrushes

Procedure

Discuss the characteristics of the pottery from each time period. Information pertaining to the details of the discovery can be found at

http://www.hiof.no/aub/aub-online/faculties/arts_
and_sciences/archaeology/index.html.

The samples uncovered appear to be from the third century BCE to the first century CE and from the fourth and fifth centuries CE. Review the span of time these unearthed artifacts represent.

Give each student a terra-cotta pot. Because the ceramics of Beirut were made of a clean, dark red material, terra-cotta pottery provides a representation of the coloring found on the pottery unearthed. Such pots can be purchased or donated by a local nursery or masonry business. The pottery should be of various shapes and sizes so that the collection is representative of the artifacts uncovered at the Beirut site.

Instruct the students to paint their terra-cotta pottery with designs similar to those found on the Islamic vessels. Because the terra-cotta surface is porous, tempera paint can be easily brushed onto the surface. Let stand overnight to dry.

The finished pieces can be exhibited for all to enjoy. Many school libraries have display cases just waiting to be filled with students' work. Arrange the "artifacts" around maps, photographs, and student reports relating to this study.

Masada, Israel

http://www.stelcom.com/inpa/masada.html
http://www.register.com/triumph/p12.htm
http://www.ior.com/~jmcmath/masada6.htm
http://www.ior.com/~jmcmath/masada2.htm

Nineteen hundred years ago, this plateau retreat, above the Judean desert and the Dead Sea, originally the winter home of King Herod, was haven to some 1,000 resisters to the Roman rampages occurring throughout this Middle Eastern land. The larger Roman army built a huge earthen ramp to the entrance of Masada, permitting troops to eventually attack in large numbers. Holding out for almost three years and seeing the cause was lost, all but a few of the remaining men, women, and children of Masada committed suicide rather than be captured and killed by the Roman army. Masada has become a symbol of spirit, courage, and love of freedom.

On this solitary mountain you will see the remains of luxurious palaces, mosaic floors, frescoes, a synagogue, bronze and silver coins, and potsherds. Centuries ago, visitors would have climbed the ominous cliffs to visit Masada. Today the visitors to this Israeli archaeological site can hike, take the cable car, or catch the Internet express.

Lesson One: Where Is the Water?

Objective

Students will become architects, designing a water- and food-storage system for the mountain fortress of Masada.

Time Required

Thirty minutes

Materials

☐ Paper with a predrawn cutaway view of the mountain of Masada

☐ Pencils and crayons

Procedures

When archaeologists reached the top of the mountainous plateau of Masada, they must have wondered how the inhabitants kept enough water and food on hand to sustain them. They discovered deep caverns within the earth that were used for food storage and as water reservoirs.

Imagine that you are one of the original architects of Masada. The community is perched atop a rock plateau hundreds of feet above the desert floor. You have to be creative in designing a water-storage system that will capture the scarce rainwater and in preserving the foods that are either gathered, grown, or hunted below.

Students can do this task either alone or in pairs. They should draw the storage systems in the cutaway view of Masada and color as desired. During the course of the project, they can share their ideas and plans with the class.

Lesson Two: Textiles of Masada

Objective

The students will perform a variety of tests on identified natural fibers found in textiles. From the results, they will compare the properties of each sample.

Time Required

One hour

Materials

- ☐ Woven fabric (wool, silk, linen, and cotton) cut into 1-by-1-inch pieces
- ☐ Bunsen burner
- ☐ Safety glasses
- ☐ Tweezers
- ☐ Microscope and slides
- ☐ Drawing paper
- ☐ Pencils

Procedure

Excavations of Masada uncovered over 3,000 textile fragments ranging from those used for clothing to those used for utilitarian purposes. The dry desert conditions of the region proved excellent for preservation. Archaeologists can analyze these finds to learn about the fashion and trade of the period.

The textiles of ancient Masada were made of natural fibers. The same type of fibers are still used in textiles. Just as scientists perform tests to discover the properties of a given sample, so can students recreate the analytical process. By comparing the results, students will observe the properties unique to each.

Provide each student with a 1-by-1-inch piece of wool, cotton, linen, and silk. Have each perform the following tests on each sample:

1. Visual Inspection

   Observe if the fabric has a luster to it. Feel the fabric. Determine if it is rough or smooth, stiff or flexible, heavy or light. Untwist the yarn and determine the length of the fiber. Instruct the students to record their observations.

2. Burning Test

   Adult supervision is necessary when performing a burning test. All participants are required to wear safety glasses. Pull several strands from the piece of fabric. Holding the strands with tweezers, slowly move them into the flame of the Bunsen burner. Does the sample burn slowly or quickly? Will the flame self-extinguish or will it continue to burn? Is the ash gray with feathery, smooth edges, or is it black and crushable? Is there an odor when burning? Students will observe how different natural fibers react differently to a flame.

3. Microscope Test

   Place a strand of fabric on a clean microscope slide. Place the cover glass on the slide and gently press down to eliminate any air bubbles. Place the slide on the stage of the microscope and adjust to focus. Draw on paper what you see through the eyepiece.

Once all four types of fibers are tested, ask the students to create charts that show the results of each test.

The Dead Sea Scrolls, Israel

http://sunsite.unc.edu/expo/deadsea.scrolls.exhibit/intro.html
http://world.std.com/~caesar/FILES/DS/facts.html

The Dead Sea Scrolls, made of leather and papyrus, contain most of the books of the Old Testament. They were discovered over several years, from 1947 to 1956, in a dark cave in the Wadi Quman in what is now the State (country) of Israel. These ancient manuscripts date back to the Essenes, a Jewish sect that lived in this area from 150 BCE to CE 68 in a settlement near the discovery site. These ancient scrolls are particularly valuable, as they take us back 2,000 years to tell about this ancient group of Palestinian Jews and how they lived. If you can't climb the hills above the Dead Sea today, visiting the Net site is the next best thing. This region is the cradle of three major religions: Christianity, Islam, and Judaism.

Lesson One: Paper Making

Objective

The history of the ancient people of Israel was preserved on the scrolls that lay hidden for thousands of years. The students will participate in the process of making paper. Using calligraphy pens, the students will write verses and phrases similar to the writings found on the Dead Sea Scrolls.

Time Required

Approximately two days
One hour each day

Materials

- ☐ Newsprint cut into strips
- ☐ Blender (one that has outlived its day in the kitchen but is great for use in the classroom; visit garage and rummage sales)
- ☐ Large spoons or ladles
- ☐ Water
- ☐ Screen mesh, stacks of newspaper, and thick books to use as weights or large bricks (two per student)
- ☐ Dull knife or spatula
- ☐ Calligraphy pens

Procedure

Ask the students to bring in newsprint from home. A 12-inch stack per group will do the trick. Tear the newsprint into small strips approximately 1 by 4 inches. Place the paper strips in an old blender. Add ½ cup water and turn on at low speed.

As the paper becomes pulp, add additional water and paper strips until the mixture takes on a pasty consistency and fills the blender. Repeat this step as needed to make enough pulp for each child in the classroom.

Select a place in the classroom to arrange the bricks or screen mesh. Cover the floor or tables with newspaper to prevent even a bigger mess in the room. Because you will need to keep this area undisturbed for two to three days while the pulped paper dries, find an area in the room that can be easily ignored.

Each student will need two bricks. Ask the local hardware store or mason to provide enough bricks for the activity. They can always be returned after the activity is completed. If this resource is not available, take screen mesh (similar to the kind used for backdoor screens) and cut large pieces to use for the activity. (We suggest you not use the screen door hanging in the teacher's lounge. Someone might notice that it is missing.)

Using a large spoon or ladle, scoop a dollop of the moistened pulp onto the top of each brick. Using fingers, the student can evenly smooth the pulp over the surface of the brick. Place the second brick on top of the smoothed pulp and apply pressure to remove the excess moisture. This procedure may be repeated as needed.

If using screen instead of the bricks, follow the same procedure of scooping and spreading the pulp. However, instead of placing bricks on the pulp, cover each dollop with a thick stack of newspaper and weigh down with five to six thick books.

Allow the top brick or books to remain stationary two to three days or until the paper has dried. Use a dull knife or spatula to free the paper from the screen.

Students can use a commercial felt tip calligraphy pen to draw images similar to those found on the scrolls.

Lesson Two: 'Tis a Puzzlement

Objective

Scholars and historians have carefully examined the fragments of the Dead Sea Scrolls and attempted to unlock history by translating the text, and theorizing as to what the missing pieces may contain. The students will participate in a simulated activity, piecing together an incomplete puzzle and determining what the missing pieces may hold.

Time Required

Twenty minutes per cooperative group

Materials

- ☐ Tabletop to build a puzzle
- ☐ Puzzle
- ☐ Writing paper
- ☐ Pens or pencils

Procedure

Select a puzzle that is appropriate for the grade level you teach. Before placing the pieces on the worktable, randomly remove 15–20 percent of the pieces, about a handful. You may want to place the removed pieces in a labeled envelope and tuck it away in the back of a desk drawer. Someday you may want to actually have the students build the completed puzzle. Don't tell them that pieces were removed from the box.

Allow each student the opportunity to work on the puzzle. After all the available pieces have been interlocked, students will discover that there are missing pieces that create gaps and fragments in the picture or design. Ask cooperative groups of students to study the available information and determine from that evidence what might be contained in the lost pieces. Instruct the groups to write down their theories and describe how they came to their conclusions. Bring the class together for discussion and comparison of the suppositions of each group. Remind students that archaeologists, scholars, and historians have spent decades studying the fragmented pieces of the scrolls in the hopes of filling in the missing pieces, just as they have done.

Tomb of Qin Shihuangdi, China:
An Army on Duty for 2,000 Years

http://www.adventure.com/library/encyclopedia/ka/rfitcarm.html
http://www.c.hiroshima-dit.ac.jp/cnetservice/10places/xian.html
http://www.hansonlib.org/bmaxian.html

In 259–210 BCE, the first emperor of ancient China, Qin Shihuangdi, ruled a turbulent land. It was Emperor Qin who connected the separate fortifications protecting China from the barbarian tribes of Mongolia into what is known as the Great Wall of China.

Some say that up to 700,000 people worked on the tomb that was begun when Qin ascended the throne of the Chinese state of Qin in 246 BCE. On the Net site you will see row after row of terra-cotta life-size soldiers guarding his tomb. Eight thousand figures of men and horses make this one of the most important archaeological finds of all time. You will also see gold, turquoise, jade jewelry, bronzes, coins, weaponry, chariots, and other amazing artifacts preserved nearly in the same condition as when they were entombed. This site offers a glimpse into the history of a powerful leader and his people.

Lesson One: Walking the Wall

Objective

Students will replicate the width of the walking surface of the Great Wall of China.

Materials

- ☐ Measuring tape or string marked off every three feet
- ☐ Sidewalk chalk

Time Required

Twenty minutes

Procedure

Imagine a great wall hundreds of miles long. In the modern world, such a feat would require giant cranes, bulldozers, huge trucks, rails, and enormous labor power. Travel back in time 2,000 years, when no modern machines existed. Yet there stands the magnificent Great Wall of China. How big is it? Can you walk on the wall? Can you drive a truck on the wall? Which U.S. president visited the wall?

Students will be shown pictures of the Great Wall of China. Some of these pictures will have size-reference items (that is, people, carts, and other objects to reference approximate size).

Ask students to estimate the width of the wall. Using the measuring tape and sidewalk chalk, students will mark on the playground an area estimated to be its width (15 to 20 feet). The students can be photographed on their "Great School Wall."

Lesson Two: Classroom Army

Objective

The students will design life-size drawings of themselves, detailing clothing and accessories of the twentieth century.

Time Required

One hour

Materials

- ☐ Roll of white butcher paper
- ☐ Marking pens, crayons, watercolor or tempera paints
- ☐ Brushes
- ☐ Scissors

Procedure

The terra-cotta clay army of the first emperor of China was made up of over 8,000 full-sized pieces. Detailed and brightly painted, these sculptures provided an outstanding depiction of an earlier time.

Give each student a piece of butcher paper that is long enough to lie down on and that extends beyond head and feet. If working with younger, smaller children, one width will suffice. Older, larger students may need to tape two widths together. Working in pairs, each student will take a turn tracing the outline of the other's body. Remind the students to hold their bodies very still, especially the arms and legs. Too much movement will cause a distortion in the tracing.

Once the body's outline is traced, students can begin to add details to their images: facial features, hairstyles, clothing, and accessories. Markers, crayons, or paints can be used to provide lively color. When the drawings are completed, students can cut them out and hang the life-size figures around the room or in a school hallway. Now instead of thirty students, you will have sixty. Oh, my!

Marki Alonia, Cyprus:
The Bronze Age

http://www.latrobe.edu.au/www/archaeology/marki/

In the Bronze Age, peoples of the world used bronze to forge tools and weapons. The Bronze Age is not a particular time but ended when the Iron Age began. In some areas this period began earlier or ended later than in others. Some civilizations bypassed it altogether. The period when bronze was used ranged from 3500 BCE to 1000 BCE.

The Marki Alonia site is located in the central area of the island of Cyprus and is dated at approximately 2300 BCE. Net visitors will see pottery, stone, metal, and other artifacts from the Bronze Age as well as excellent photographs of the site, the archaeological team, and the land.

Lesson One: Tic-Tac-Toe in the Bronze Age (or Sticks and Rocks)

Objective

Students will construct and play a simple game. Perhaps its origins are in this ancient civilization.

Time Required

From the Bronze Age to the Iron Age (Just kidding!) About ten minutes for each game

Materials

☐ Three 2-inch sticks

☐ Three rocks

☐ Tic-tac-toe gameboard drawn in the sand or dirt (or drawn with chalk on the playground blacktop)

Procedure

Draw a tic-tac-toe board in the sand or dirt. You can also use chalk to draw the board on the blacktop of the playground.

Each of the two players gets either the three rocks or the three sticks. The first player lays a stick in a space, the second player a rock. This continues until all the pieces are on the board. The next move requires that the player whose turn it is lifts one of the pieces and places it somewhere else. This is followed by the other player doing the same. This action continues until one player has the sticks or rocks all in a row (just like tic-tac-toe). When that happens, the game is over. This is a game you can play anywhere, even during a rock concert ... or is that a bronze concert?

Lesson Two: Properties of Metal

Objective

Students will compare various properties of several metals that represent different periods in technological development.

Time Required

Forty-five minutes

Materials

- ☐ Measured rods (½–2 inches) of bronze, iron, copper, aluminum
- ☐ Balance scale with weights
- ☐ Paper
- ☐ Pencils
- ☐ Watch(es) with a second hand
- ☐ Tank of water

Procedure

Purchase metal rods at an area welding supply shop or steelyard. Let the proprietor know what you are doing, and ask for a donation. The metal should all be the same diameter and cut to the same length. This may be done at the supply store, or a parent with metal-working skills can prepare the metal beforehand. Be sure that any sharp edges have been smoothed and rounded.

Divide the class into groups of three students. Each group will 1) measure the rods to determine that they are indeed the same length and diameter and record these numbers (it can be pointed out that it's important to begin with pieces that are the same size), 2) weigh each rod and record the weight, 3) carefully drop each metal sample in a tank of water and record the time it takes to reach the bottom.

The students then should be able to make conclusions about each metal in relation to the others. Groups can compare their findings.

As an extension activity, students can research the periodic table and determine molecular properties of each type of metal. Or they can make lists of the common uses for each of the metals, for example, copper is used for wire (as a conductor of electricity), and iron is used in the manufacture of automobile parts.

Petra, Jordan:
The City Carved from Rock

http://www.activelife.com/jordan/
http://www.mit.edu:8001/activities/jordanians/jordan/petra.html

Imagine site-seeing in the streets of the ancient city of Petra, where 800 individual monuments were carved from pink sandstone by Nabataean artisans. Carved into the salmon-colored cliffs are temples, royal tombs, a Roman-style theater, houses, markets, public buildings, and paved streets. Petra thrived for 400 years—carrying on trade with other wealthy cities in Greece, Rome, Egypt, and Syria—until it was occupied by Roman legions in CE 106. Truly, Petra is one of the great wonders of the world. It certainly is a wonder for *Dig That Site*. Be sure to visit the several Petra links that showcase this amazing old city.

Lesson One: Paved Streets in the Desert

Objective

Students will reenact the ancient process of street paving using rocks or bricks.

Time Required

Thirty minutes

Materials

- ☐ String
- ☐ Four stakes, about 2 feet long
- ☐ Approximately 100 rocks
- ☐ Shovel(s) and broom(s)
- ☐ Sand
- ☐ Water

Procedures

One of the signs of a great civilization is paved streets, which allowed pedestrians and vehicles to move about more easily. Streets in ancient cities were quite different from the asphalt or concrete roadways of modern cities. They were paved with stone. Many examples of such stone-paved streets can be seen throughout the world.

Have each student bring a rock to school (diameter of 6–8 inches). Be sure to instruct students on the safety issues related to the transportation of these objects.

Discuss the basics of paving (selecting similar-sized stones, running a level line, placing the stones, securing the stones, etc.). Find a suitable place on the schoolground where you can pave an area perhaps 6 by 4 feet.

Dig out the area approximately 3 inches deep.

Set a level line between the wooden stakes to ensure the paving will be fairly level and suitable for walking or vehicles. To set a level line, first drive four stakes into the ground, one at each corner of the area to be paved. Drive the stakes deep enough so that they stand solidly—about halfway into the ground should do it. Be sure the stakes are fairly straight. Then tie a string from one stake to another around the perimeter of the dug-out area. Students may either use a line level (a small, inexpensive device available from hardware stores) or may "eyeball" the string to make sure it is straight.

Have students create the paving by placing rocks in the recessed area, matching them so the paving is without large gaps and is level. Students may need to dig out or fill in the spaces under the rocks to make the paved area level.

When the area is fully paved and level, fill the spaces between the rocks with sand, decomposed granite, or dirt. Sweep excess into the spaces. Sprinkle water over the path to settle the dirt and secure the rocks. You now have engaged in the ancient art of paving.

Lesson Two: Carved Buildings

Objective

The ancient city of Petra was carved from the sandstone hills of Jordan. Using Styrofoam and woodworking files, the students will carve buildings to create a carved city of their own.

Time Required

Two hours

Materials

- ☐ Large sheets of 3-inch-thick Styrofoam
- ☐ Assortment of woodworking files
- ☐ Serrated knife
- ☐ Red, white, and yellow tempera paint
- ☐ Paintbrushes

Procedure

Because of the texture of the Styrofoam, use a serrated knife to saw the larger pieces into individual sections. This should be done by the teacher prior to the distribution of the materials to the class. Cut in 12-by-12-inch pieces.

Ask students to bring in woodworking files from home. These are available in many sizes and will be used to mold and shape the Styrofoam into the facades of the buildings.

In learning groups of dyads or triads, the students will discuss and design a structure that will become part of their city. View the images of Petra on the Internet, discussing the types of buildings found at this site.

Instruct the students to begin carving the city. This is done by carefully filing the edges of the Styrofoam to form the top of the structure. The front of the building can be molded by pressing the sharper end of the file into the Styrofoam, creating indented portions that take on the look of pillars, arches, and decorative walls.

Following the carving of the city, instruct the students to paint the Styrofoam a salmon color so that it appears similar to the Petra site. Mix red and white tempera paint to create pink. Slowly add yellow to the mixture, a small portion at a time, until a salmon color is achieved. Paint the facade of the Styrofoam buildings with the salmon-colored paint. Place the finished pieces side by side on a shelf or anchor them on a bulletin board using t-pins.

Europe

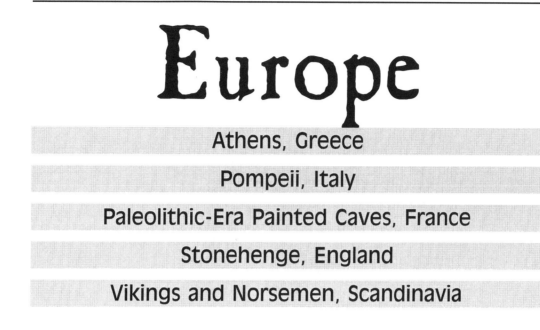

Athens, Greece

Pompeii, Italy

Paleolithic-Era Painted Caves, France

Stonehenge, England

Vikings and Norsemen, Scandinavia

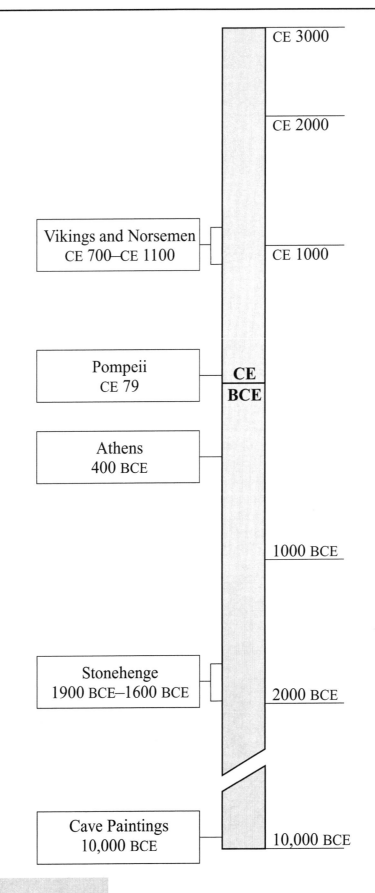

CE 3000

CE 2000

Vikings and Norsemen
CE 700–CE 1100

CE 1000

Pompeii
CE 79

CE
BCE

Athens
400 BCE

1000 BCE

Stonehenge
1900 BCE–1600 BCE

2000 BCE

Cave Paintings
10,000 BCE

10,000 BCE

Timeline for Europe

From *Dig That Site: Exploring Archaeology, History, and Civilization on the Internet.*
© 1997. Gary M. Garfield and Suzanne McDonough. Libraries Unlimited. (800) 237-6124.

Europe

The modern civilizations of Canada, the United States, Latin America, Australia, and New Zealand developed largely from European culture. Europe occupies the western fifth of the world's largest land mass, which is shared with Asia. Europe reaches to the Arctic Ocean in the north, the Mediterranean Sea in the south, the Atlantic Ocean in the west, and what was once the Soviet Union in the east. The earliest of the European civilizations occurred around 3000 BCE on the islands in the Aegean Sea east of Greece. Our young archaeologists will move across the European continent in search of ancient civilizations.

1. Athens, Greece
2. Pompeii, Italy
3. Paleolithic-Era Painted Caves, France
4. Stonehenge, England
5. Vikings and Norsemen, Scandinavia

From *Dig That Site: Exploring Archaeology, History, and Civilization on the Internet.*
© 1997. Gary M. Garfield and Suzanne McDonough. Libraries Unlimited. (800) 237-6124.

Athens, Greece

http://www.indiana.edu/~kglowack/Athens/Athens.html

The Athenian days of greatest glory date back to the 400s BCE, when Athens was the most powerful city in the world.

The visitor to the Athens archaeological site will view beautiful reconstructed temples, ruins, and other antiquities such as the Acropolis, which translates as "high city." In modern Athens, many of the ancient treasures are in the city's fine museums, but the streets and many squares, the open-air market tucked below the Acroplis, and the many street vendors echo the active street life of the ancient city. The site provides an opportunity for the student of ancient peoples to step back from the pages of textbooks and enter the tapestry of Athens that is part yesterday, part tomorrow.

Lesson One: Sandwiches with Socrates

One of the passions of Greeks in both ancient and modern Athens is lively conversation and good food. This activity will enable our field archaeologists to experience at least one of these passions.

Objective

The students will prepare Greek sandwiches.

Time Required

One hour

Materials

- ☐ Pita bread or pocket bread
- ☐ A host of optional ingredients (see instructions below)
- ☐ Spoons

Procedure

First get one of those big white chef hats and an apron, and you'll soon be cooking. A toga is nice but not necessary. Actually, old long-sleeved men's or women's dress shirts will do fine. Get a few parents to assist you in this lesson, and you'll more likely be eating Greek food instead of picking it up off the floor. You may want to do this in a center format or as a simple serving line as lunch time nears.

Provide a variety of ingredients from which the students can choose. These should include lettuce, olives (Greek olives would be nice), cucumbers, sliced meat, softened chick peas, marinated artichoke hearts, feta cheese, and just about anything you fancy when pushing the cart down the supermarket aisles. Make an appealing white sauce from garlic, lemon juice, and ground potatoes or simply use a Ranch-style salad dressing.

Line up all the ingredients, starting with the plates and pita bread (slice off the top so that an opening is big enough to spoon in the ingredients) and saving the sauces for last. The students will pick up the pocket bread and make selections from the ingredients on the table. Use spoons to assist in the pocket filling. Be sure to instruct the students to take only small portions so the bread will not split open. Everyone should enjoy these reminders of the past.

For those who wish a healthy accompaniment, make a Greek salad using a variety of lettuce greens, black olives, firm tomatoes, sweet red onions, and of course, lots of feta cheese. A very colorful gastronomic delight.

Lesson Two: Architecture in Ancient Athens

Objective

The students will learn about the architecture of ancient Athens, particularly the use of columns in the magnificent temple structures. Experimenting with a variety of building materials, the students will construct three identical columns and subject them to specific tests. From their observations, the students will discover how the ancient columns were engineered and why they have withstood the passage of time.

Time Required

One hour

Materials

☐ A variety of building materials:
interlocking plastic blocks
wooden or plastic blocks
small empty boxes
paper towel tubes
aluminum cans

☐ Cardboard

☐ Heavy objects (textbook, rock, or the like)

☐ Spray bottle filled with water

☐ Electric fan

Procedure

Introduce the students to the city of Athens by viewing the images available on the Web site. Explore the Acropolis and its buildings, and visit the Parthenon.

Focus the attention of the students on the use of columns in the architecture of the ancient Greeks. Discuss the function of columns. How were they used for structural support? What decorative role did they serve?

As an inquiry lesson, ask the students to think about how the columns were built to ensure strength and stability in the architectural structure. Provide them with a variety of building materials, and instruct them to build three identical columns. When the columns are completed, position them on a movable cardboard base, but do not secure them.

Put each set of pillars to the following tests:

1. Place a heavy object on top of the capitals of the pillars.

2. Gently shake the foundation board.

3. Subject the columns to weather conditions (use a spray bottle filled with water and an electric fan to simulate rain and wind).

When the testing is complete, observe which designs withstood the conditions and remained in an upright position. Discuss the characteristics of those that were left standing and those that were destroyed. Draw conclusions as to how the ancient Greek architects designed their columns, what materials were used, and how they were constructed.

As a follow-up activity, the students can study the early column designs. The Greeks developed three basic types of columns: Doric, Ionic, and Corinthian. Some were highly ornamental, others simple. All features of the columns served a purpose. From the research, the students can surmise why their columns either collapsed or remained standing.

Pompeii, Italy

http://enterzone.berkeley.edu/ez/e2/articles/frankel/tourlist.html
http://www.theplumber.com/pom.html
http://jefferson.village.virginia.edu/pompeii/page-1.html

In CE 79, Mount Vesuvius erupted suddenly, covering the town of Pompeii with hot ash, poison gas, and suffocating smoke. Thousands were killed where they slept or as they fled the dying city. The hot, wet ash settled, encasing and sealing the city for almost 1,700 years. It was not until the 1500s that city workers broke into Pompeii, rediscovering her riches. During the next 400 years, Pompeii would be studied and excavated. Even today, the excavation continues as archaeologists attempt to learn more about this wondrous place near the Mediterranean Sea.

The Pompeii Web site sheds light on the life and times of the residents of Pompeii who perished in the ash-covered city. You will travel down the cobblestone streets, into the courtyards, beneath the arches, and into the living quarters in this city where a great civilization once flourished.

Lesson One: The Excavation of Ash

Objective

Students will construct a shoe-box city, recreating the burial of Pompeii. Tell students to bring smocks or old clothes to wear for this activity.

Time Required

One hour for construction
Thirty minutes for the simulation

Materials

- ☐ Shoe boxes
- ☐ Clear cellophane paper
- ☐ Large boxes or newspapers
- ☐ Colored construction paper
- ☐ Glue or tape
- ☐ Small plants and twigs
- ☐ Several buckets of ash collected from the fireplace, barbecue, or campfire. Be sure the ash is cold! Also, tell students to bring smocks or old clothes to wear for this activity.
- ☐ Sifter or strainer (optional)

Procedure

Provide each group of four with one shoe box.

Instruct the students to cut a window in one of the long sides of the box and glue in a piece of cellophane paper. Cover the other sides of the box with colored construction paper. (Leave the top open.) Have students make small buildings, bridges, streets, walls, wells, and aqueducts out of construction paper or other suitable materials. Students can use small plants and twigs for the vegetation. Glue or tape the objects in place to simulate a mini-Pompeii.

After the glue has dried, set the shoe box in a larger box or on newspaper *outside* the building. Holding a container of fine ash 3 feet in the air, begin sprinkling the ash onto the shoe-box city. Students can use a sifter-strainer or slowly drop by hand. The city does not need to be completely covered; students can observe through the cellophane paper and from the top what happens. Many of the "buildings" will collapse. Students can surmise that the city will be cut off from light and air, suffocating all who remain inside.

Put the lid on the box and display the ash-covered city in the classroom for all to see. Variations are acceptable!

Lesson Two: A Story Entombed

Objective

The students will simulate how the imprinting of objects occurred within the entombed and hardened volcanic ash.

Time Required

Three thirty-minute sessions

Materials

- ☐ A balloon for each two students
- ☐ Pieces of string 5 inches long
- ☐ Glue sticks
- ☐ Plaster of paris
- ☐ Miscellaneous objects such as scrap paper, coins, pebbles, leaves, and fabric scraps
- ☐ Newspaper
- ☐ Long pin or long, thin nail

Procedures

Much of the evidence discovered in the ruins of Pompeii had been entombed by hot, wet ash, which formed a tight case around the object. Many centuries later, when archaeologists opened the hard ash enclosures, they found only the imprint of the original object that had perished in the disaster. These imprints provided much information about the lives and deaths of the inhabitants of Pompeii.

Each team of students is given a small balloon, string, and a handful of miscellaneous objects. One student blows up the balloon (to the point that it is not full) and ties off the end using the string. Using the glue stick, students attach ten or fifteen of the paper scraps, objects, and coins (pennies won't break you) to the outside of the balloon. Set aside until stuck! Demonstrate how to mix the plaster into the consistency of soft peanut butter (don't use peanut butter). Over the newspaper, students cover the balloon until it is encased with at least an inch of plaster. This may take several applications, letting each coat dry.

After the entire object has dried, slowly insert the pin or nail. The air from the balloon should escape. Now break open the plaster, remove the miscellaneous items and the deflated balloon. Notice that imprints of the objects placed against the balloon remain. Observe that the cavity is the same shape as the balloon. Display the artifacts with signs describing the process. You may wish to photograph the steps for a display board.

Paleolithic-Era Painted Caves, France

http://mistral.culture.fr/culture/gvpda-en.htm

The Paleolithic era, or Old Stone Age, is the period when humans first appeared and evolved into early hunters and farmers. We have learned much about these early people through archaeological sites where the refuse left behind provides clues to their life and ways. Among these people was the artist of Pont-d'Arc, who left a legacy for modern man. The mystery of what occurred in these cave art galleries is being slowly unraveled as scientists continue their study into this magnificent monument from the last ice age.

On the Web site, you will explore the dark, damp corridors that lead to a vast underground network of caves that have held captive the decorations, paintings, and engravings dating from the Paleolithic era (that's a long time ago). The visitor will view paintings of bison, lions, horses, rhinoceroses, wild oxen, bears, panthers, mammoths, owls, and many other animals. Along with the paintings, evidence of humans can be found in pieces of carved flint, traces of torches, arrangements of stone, and the placement of animal remains.

Lesson One: Inside the Caves

Objective

Cro-Magnon humans used minerals found in the area to create the cave paintings found in France. Students will identify three of the minerals and use them to create their own decorated tile.

Time Required

One hour

Materials

☐ One mineral sample per student of each of the following:
   iron manganese
   yellow ochre (limonite)
   red ochre (hematite)

☐ One 4-by-4-inch white, nonglossy tile

☐ One calcite mineral sample (to be used as a visual aid)

Procedure

Have students view the images of early cave paintings via the Internet. Discuss possible theories as to how and by whom the cave paintings were made.

Purchase mineral samples from a local rock shop or related businesses. Distribute the mineral samples to each student. Ask students to list the properties of each. Let them look at the color, feel the weight, test the hardness, and so on. Provide background information about the minerals:

1. Early humans used yellow ochre, red ochre, and black iron manganese to create the cave paintings.

2. These minerals are naturally formed in rock.

3. All are iron rich.

4. Many of the cavern walls and paintings are encrusted with calcite, which has preserved them.

Instruct the students to create their own painting by gently scratching the surface of the tile; fragments of the minerals will remain on the tile's surface. Use all three minerals to add color and depth to the drawings. Designs should depict wildlife so that they are similar to those created by early humans.

Lesson Two: Classroom Cave Painting

Objective

In a darkened classroom, the students will draw pictures that depict surroundings or interests. They will use flashlights as their only source of light so that they can experience what it might have been like for Cro-Magnon people to create their cave paintings in darkened caverns.

Time Required

Forty-five minutes

Materials

- ☐ Butcher paper or large sheets of drawing paper
- ☐ Crayons, markers, or chalk
- ☐ Three to five flashlights
- ☐ Dark paper or aluminum foil

Procedure

The cavern walls found in Lascaux and Ardèche are decorated with paintings and engravings dating from the Paleolithic era. These caves provide evidence for the activities of early humans. Carefully placed animal remains, carved flint, arrangements of stones and traces of torches provide a picture of how and why the ancient galleries were created. Point out to the students that because caves are dark, torches played an important role.

Prior to the day's lesson, cover classroom windows with dark paper or aluminum foil. This will reduce the amount of light that can enter the room. On designated walls, hang large pieces of butcher paper or drawing paper for the students' artwork.

Have the class work in cooperative groups. Instruct the students to create images that depict their lifestyles and/or interests. These can range from skateboarding to swimming, watching television, or shopping at the mall or can be pictures of superheroes or movie stars. Give each group one flashlight. Instruct students that it will be their only source of light.

When each group has been assigned its designated area, instruct the "holder of the torch" (flashlight) to turn it on. At this time, the teacher will turn off the classroom lights so that the room is darkened and the decorating can begin. Students may use crayons, markers, or chalk to create their pictures.

When the paintings are finished and the lights are turned on, have the students share their images. These pictures can later adorn the bulletin boards or hallway galleries for all to enjoy.

Stonehenge, England

http://www2.ucsc.edu/people/trillian/stonehenge/start.html
http://www.gold.net/users/iy12/aaes/astroarc.htm
http://avebury.arch.soton.ac.uk/LocalStuff/Stonehenge/stonehenge.html

Stonehenge, located on the Salisbury Plain in England, is a circular structure of huge stones that are not indigenous to the area. The arrangement of the stones has puzzled scientists for centuries and has been a source of amazement for those who visit. Who built this unusual structure and for what purpose? Is it a monument to the gods or an ancient observatory capable of predicting astronomical events? Scientists believe it was constructed between 1900 BCE and 1600 BCE. (Who knew we would be counting backward!) "Net walk" around this magnificent relic from a past civilization and become part of the Stonehenge scientific community. Many say Stonehenge is the eighth wonder of the ancient world. You decide.

Lesson One: How Were the Stones Moved and Raised?

Objective

Students will participate in moving objects that defy normal human strength by using rollers, levers, and other devices.

Time Required

Forty-five minutes

Materials

- ☐ Six bricks per group
- ☐ Ten pieces of dowel (6 inches long; ¼ to ½ inch in diameter) per group
- ☐ Three pieces of dowel (12 inches long by ½ inch in diameter) per group
- ☐ String
- ☐ Pencils and paper

Procedure

Students as a class can engage in an inquiry regarding how the stones must have been brought to this site. The teacher will explain that these stones were far too heavy for humans to carry or pull in conventional ways.

Breaking the students into groups of three, provide each group with six bricks, dowels (long and short), and string. Ask each group to simulate how the builders of Stonehenge moved, and then lifted, the stones into place. After students have demonstrated this to the teacher, they can illustrate their findings for later discussion. Encourage creativity. If the ideas of rollers, pulleys, and levers do not surface, the teacher can introduce them to the class.

Lesson Two: The Meaning of Stonehenge

Objective

Students will utilize the Internet and other resources to discover the "meaning" of Stonehenge.

Time Required

Two forty-five-minute sessions

Materials

- ☐ Internet resources
- ☐ Library books and reserved books
- ☐ Writing materials
- ☐ Butcher paper

Procedure

Define the problem for the students: What is the meaning of Stonehenge? Explain or review research techniques related to the Internet and/or conventional resources. Divide the students into cooperative groups of three to four. Discuss the strategies for working together in this setting, for example, brainstorming, assigning tasks, sharing task progress, sharing data collection, making assumptions, and drawing conclusions.

Monitor the students as they move into their tasks. Assist and facilitate with resources so that progress is continuous. Offer appropriate reinforcement for success and provide encouragement to maintain progress.

When each group feels that it has reached a theory or a conclusion, instruct the students to write their hypotheses on the large butcher-paper chart hanging in the front of the room. They should include a description of the rationale and evidence for the conclusions. When all groups have completed the task, instruct each to make an oral presentation explaining its rationale.

Following the presentations, have a feedback session to ascertain how the process worked for the students.

Vikings and Norsemen, Scandinavia

http://www.demon.co.uk/history/index.html
http://www.sound.net/~billhoyt/kensington.htm

Between the late 700s and 1100s, the Vikings explored the North Atlantic in advanced ships, reaching as far away as the Americas. These northern European warriors were fierce, looting and conquering parts of England, France, Germany, Ireland, Italy, Russia, and Spain. There is speculation and some evidence suggesting that the Vikings may have explored North America hundreds of years prior to the expeditions of Christopher Columbus. Sail into this site and learn more about the history, ships, and artifacts of these feared explorers.

Lesson One: Shipbuilding and Sailing: A Way of Life

Objective

Students will design, build, and test-sail aluminum foil Viking ships.

Time Required

One hour

Materials

- ☐ Aluminum foil
- ☐ A bucket of pennies
- ☐ Large plastic trough (outside) filled two-thirds with water

Procedure

The sea nearly surrounds the northern European area where the Vikings lived, and with the preponderance of fjords along the coastline, it was natural that the water was an important means of transportation and commerce for these people.

Distribute to each student one precut square-foot sheet of aluminum foil. Instruct students to carefully fold and shape "Viking" ships and position two or three pennies in the bottom of each boat to act as ballast. They can test-float their Viking ships in the trough of water. If a vessel sinks, direct the student to make an adaptation in the design. For a variation, students can test the boats for strength by filling them with more pennies and increasing the weight.

Lesson Two: The Kensington Rune Stone

Objective

The students will collect evidence about the Kensington rune stone. They will hold a debate as to whether it is an authentic Viking rune stone or a forgery.

Time Required

Two one-hour sessions

Materials

☐ Encyclopedias

☐ History books about the Vikings

☐ Internet resources

Procedure

The Kensington rune stone has been the subject of scholarly debate since its discovery in 1898. Found by a Swedish immigrant on his farm in Kensington, Minnesota, the stone slab is believed to be a rune stone containing an account of Norse explorers in the fourteenth century. Many scholars have examined the rune stone. Some call it a fraud; others claim it to be authentic.

If the stone is genuine, this would mean that the era of Norse exploration lasted centuries longer than previously thought and that these early adventurers explored large areas of the North American continent. If it is a fake, the Kensington rune stone remains one of the best archaeological pranks.

Let your students set the record straight. Divide the class into two groups. Group 1 will gather evidence to support that the Kensington stone is authentic. Group 2 will try to uncover the hoax and provide proof to support its findings. Select a leader for each group who is responsible for delegating tasks and ensuring that each member of the group participates in the presentation. Roles may include key speakers, chart makers, typists, and artists. All students can contribute to the project in their area of strength.

Select a distinguished group to sit on a panel. Traveling colleagues, the superintendent, principal, and parents are good choices. Students will make their presentations and debate the issues. Following the debate, the panel will meet and come to a consensus. The scholars have not been able to reach closure on the issue. It will be interesting to see what the panel decides.

Africa

The Pyramids of Giza, Egypt

The Great Enclosure, Zimbabwe

Young Tut's Tomb, Egypt

Carthage, Tunisia

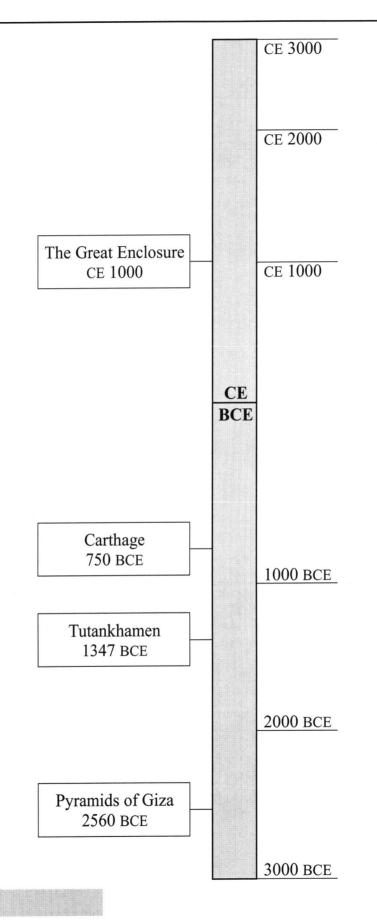

CE 3000

CE 2000

The Great Enclosure
CE 1000

CE 1000

CE
BCE

Carthage
750 BCE

1000 BCE

Tutankhamen
1347 BCE

2000 BCE

Pyramids of Giza
2560 BCE

3000 BCE

Timeline for Africa

From *Dig That Site: Exploring Archaeology, History, and Civilization on the Internet.*
© 1997. Gary M. Garfield and Suzanne McDonough. Libraries Unlimited. (800) 237-6124.

Africa

Africa is a land of great contrasts and diversity, encompassing tropical rain forests and the world's largest desert, beautiful ocean beaches, and snow-covered mountains. The people, 70 percent of whom reside in rural areas, reflect Africa's rich legacy of a wide variety of religious beliefs and ethnic backgrounds. Africa is the second-largest continent in area and the third largest in population. It is divided into more than fifty independent countries. We will explore this mysterious continent.

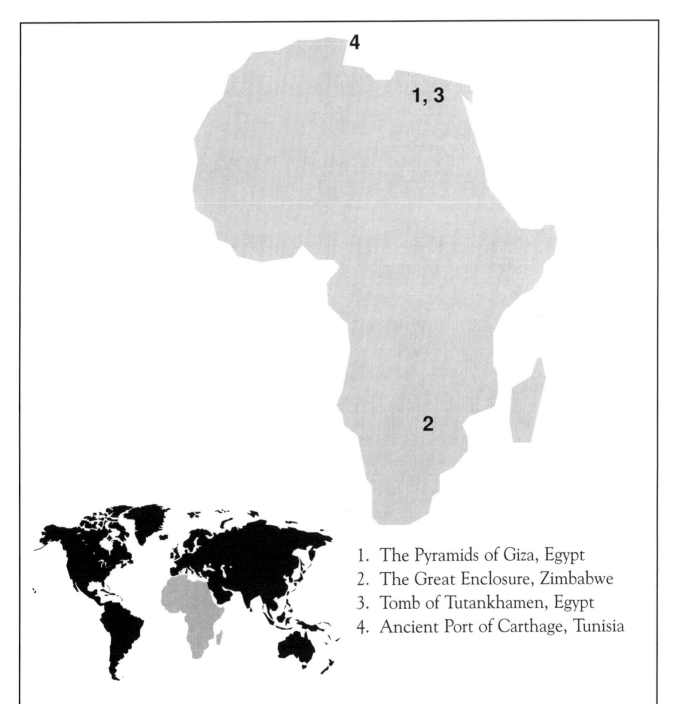

1. The Pyramids of Giza, Egypt
2. The Great Enclosure, Zimbabwe
3. Tomb of Tutankhamen, Egypt
4. Ancient Port of Carthage, Tunisia

The Pyramids of Giza, Egypt

http://pharos.bu.edu/Egypt/Wonders/pyramid.html
http://galaxy.cau.edu/tsmith/Gpyr.html
http://199.182.229.110/Exhibits/ADAE/fig23d.htm

The great pyramid of the Egyptian pharaoh Khufu of the Fourth Dynasty (2560 BCE) was constructed over a twenty-year period to serve as his tomb upon his death. Many ideas and theories exist as to how the giant stone blocks were moved to the site and raised to the heights required. On the Web site, students will climb the steps of the great pyramids of Giza and learn about one of the majestic and mysterious seven wonders of the ancient world. They will walk the sands of ancient Memphis to view the great tomb known as the pyramid of Khufu. Our young visitors will learn about the lives of the pharaohs and the beliefs that required them to build these monuments for their final journey. Linked pages show cutaway sections and breathtaking aerial photographs of the Giza Plateau.

Lesson One: The Architect's Design

Objective

Following a discussion, readings, and viewing of the interior of the Giza pyramids, students will design a vandal-proof central burial chamber.

Time Required

One hour

Materials

- ☐ Drawing paper
- ☐ Pencils
- ☐ Straightedge
- ☐ Crayons

Procedure

The teacher will discuss with the students efforts made by the pyramid architects to protect the king from robbers and looters by designing impenetrable tunnels, traps, and dead ends. Show students architectural drawings of various structures.

Instruct our young archaeologists/pyramid designers to make a drawing of a unique pyramid with innovative devices for keeping out looters. Encourage them to be very clever in their designs and to remember that their purpose is to protect the king for centuries to come.

Students should label the chambers and protective devices and post their drawings for all to see.

Lesson Two: The Geometry of the Pyramids

Objective

The students will discover the geometrical concepts used to construct the ancient Egyptian pyramids. Using this information, they will construct a tag-board pyramid.

Time Required

One hour

Materials

- ☐ Tag board
- ☐ Rulers
- ☐ Protractors
- ☐ Pencils
- ☐ Paper
- ☐ Tape

Procedure

In geometry, a pyramid is defined as a solid figure with triangular faces that meet at a common point. The number of sides on the base determines the number of triangular faces on the pyramid. For example, if the base polygon has four sides, the pyramid will have four faces; if the base has five sides, there are five faces. The pyramids of ancient Egypt had a square base and four triangular sides.

Ask students to study the shape of the pyramids of Giza. Define the following terms as they relate to the geometric shape: base, face, vertex, altitude, polygon, and congruent. From the information gathered, instruct the students to design and construct a pyramid.

Using a ruler, draw a four-inch square on the tag board. This is only a guide. You may want the students to begin with a larger or smaller base. This square will serve as the foundation polygon for the pyramid. Be sure that the sides are congruent and the angles measure ninety degrees.

Now draw four equilateral triangles whose sides measure the length of one side of the square. You may want the students to measure the angles with a protractor and record the findings, thus further defining the meaning of equilateral. Cut out the shapes. Tape the pieces together to form a pyramid.

As a follow-up language arts activity, ask students to write the procedure for the construction of their pyramids. Emphasize the use of geometric terms and step-by-step directions.

The Great Enclosure, Zimbabwe

http://wn.apc.org/mediatech/VRZ10011.HTM
http://wn.apc.org/mediatech/tourism/tn08000b.htm

Zimbabwe, a landlocked country in southeast Africa, is rich in archaeological history. Bushman paintings and various tools discovered offer evidence that Stone Age people lived in this region. Although the history of Zimbabwe is long and rich, our focus will be on the Shona people of CE 1000, who are responsible for the city that they called Great Zimbabwe, or "house of stone." We will visit what is known as the Iron Age site with its remains of this extensive town built between CE 1200 and CE 1450. The stone walls, approximately twenty feet thick and thirty-six feet high, are built with granite blocks without the use of mortar. The Net visitor will see photographs of the conical tower as well as the enclosure that required some one million granite blocks for construction. In this archaeological journey into Africa, we study a most unusual early community.

Lesson One: Flora and Fauna of Zimbabwe

Objective

Mufaro's Beautiful Daughters: An African Tale by John Steptoe retells a folktale of Africa. The ancient enclosure of Great Zimbabwe, its flora, and its fauna are the inspiration for the illustrations. Following the reading of the story and a discussion of the illustrations, the students will list the animals and plant life depicted in the story. From the list, the students will research a specific topic.

Time Required

Two sessions, one hour each

Materials

☐ *Mufaro's Beautiful Daughters: An African Tale* by John Steptoe
☐ Reference books
☐ Internet resources

Procedure

Read aloud *Mufaro's Beautiful Daughters: An African Tale* by John Steptoe. Ask the students to pay close attention to the illustrations in the story. Inform them that the setting of the story is the ancient city of Great Zimbabwe and that the plant and animal life depicted are indigenous to this region of Africa.

Following the reading of the story, have the students list and identify the flora and fauna depicted in the story. Use traditional research sources such as the library, encyclopedia, and science books to identify the plants and animals. Allow the students to explore the infinite online resources. Visit biology and botany departments of universities around the world, search databases, and contact experts in the field by e-mail for additional information. Use Internet search engines to facilitate the collection of information. (See the introduction for specific instructions.)

After researching the topic and collecting the information, the students can present their findings. Traditional methods such as research papers are acceptable; however, encourage nontraditional presentations as well. Computer multimedia presentations can be created using such programs as HyperStudio, ClarisWorks, or PowerPoint.

Lesson Two: The Great Enclosure

Objective

Within Great Zimbabwe stood the structure known as the Great Enclosure. It is estimated that it was composed of almost 1 million granite blocks. Using stones and rocks of various sizes, students will explore the concept of 1 million.

Time Required

One hour

Materials

- ☐ Stones and rocks of various sizes
- ☐ Rulers, metric or standard
- ☐ Calculators
- ☐ Pencils
- ☐ Paper

Procedure

Bring an array of stones and rocks into the classroom. These can be brought from home, collected from the school playground, or provided by the teacher. They should range in size from being just a few centimeters in length to measuring many inches. Divide these among cooperative groups. Each group should be given three rocks, each a different size: one small, one medium, and one large.

Instruct the students to measure their three sample rocks. You may need to specify which number system to use, either standard or metric, depending on your preference, and the types of measuring tools you are using.

Demonstrate how to measure the rocks. Place the rock on a piece of plain white paper. Using a pencil, trace the perimeter. Remove the rock and set it aside. Using a ruler, determine the widest part of the outline. Place points at each end. Draw a line between the two points; then measure the distance. Record the number for later use.

Using the three measurements obtained by their group, students will perform the following tasks:

1. Calculate how long a single line of stones would be if 1 million of a given size were laid one next to the other. Do this for all three samples.

2. Calculate how many more stones would be needed in order to make the two shorter distances equal to the longest distance.

3. Write word problems using the information and numbers provided in the activity.

Young Tut's Tomb, Egypt

http://pami.uwaterloo.ca/~reda/kings/kings.html
http://www1.usa1.com/~madartis/EGYPT/EGYPT.html
http://www1.usa1.com/~madartis/EGYPT/alphabet.html

Tutankhamen lived for a mere 18 years. He reigned over ancient Egypt for only nine years, from 1347 BCE to 1339 BCE. This site reveals the thousands of artifacts that were either used by the young king or placed in his four-room burial tomb to be carried with him to the next life. The tomb contained more than 5,000 objects including lifelike gold-covered masks, beds, linens, chairs, swords, daggers, shields, trumpets, fans, and statues. Because the young Tutankhamen's tomb remained undiscovered for centuries after his death and was not plundered by grave robbers, the artifacts proved to be a true archaeological treasure. Everything that was placed in the tomb when the young king died in 1339 BCE remained where it had been left. Just as the British archaeologist Howard Carter, who discovered this tomb in 1922, must have stood in amazement at what he had found, you too, can marvel at this visual feast of ancient history.

Lesson One: If I Were Pharaoh

Objective

Using the Internet, students will learn about King Tutankhamen and his tomb and write an essay as to what it would be like to be a child king or queen.

Time Required

One and one-half hours

Materials

- ☐ Internet resources
- ☐ Paper
- ☐ Pencils

Procedure

Ask students to think about what it would be like to be a leader of a country at their age. Discuss the advantages and disadvantages. Focus the discussion on such topics as power, control, isolation from peers, decision making, treatment by others, wealth, and precautions for one's own safety.

Following the discussion, instruct the students to write an essay about what it would be like to be a child king or queen. Include issues covered in the discussion. They should follow the steps of the writing process: brainstorm, write a rough draft, edit and produce the final copy. Students can then read aloud their essay for all to enjoy.

Lesson Two: Ancient Egyptian Hieroglyphics

Objective

The students will learn the fundamental concepts of ancient Egyptian hieroglyphics. Each student will create a hieroglyph that represents his or her own name.

Time Required

One and one-half hours

Materials

- ☐ Internet resources or traditional resources
- ☐ Permanent black marking pens
- ☐ Parchment-colored drawing paper
- ☐ Watercolors
- ☐ Paintbrushes

Procedure

Provide the students with the following background on Egyptian hieroglyphics:

The earliest known samples depict pictorial characters and used exact images to represent a specific subject.

There are nearly 700 symbols in Egyptian hieroglyphics.

The presentation of the hieroglyphs indicated the order in which the writing was to be read. For example, if the hieroglyphs were in columns, they were read from top to bottom.

Hieroglyphs were carved from stone or written on papyrus.

Brilliant colors were sometimes used.

If the hieroglyph represented the name of a person, it was surrounded by a cartouche, or oval ring.

The Rosetta Stone provided the means for deciphering Egyptian hieroglyphs and thus revealed to scholars the history of ancient Egypt.

Provide students with samples of the Egyptian alphabet. This can be downloaded from the Internet using the provided URLs or viewed in traditional resource books obtained at the library.

Students will write their names using Egyptian hieroglyphs. Once they have sketched their designs, they can transfer them to the paper using the permanent black marker to outline the design. Remind the students to encircle their pictures with a cartouche (oval), since the hieroglyphs represent names. Using watercolors, they can add color to the images.

As a variation on the lesson, instruct the students to create the hieroglyphs at home and bring the projects in on an assigned date with the front covered so that no one knows who the creator might be. Hang the hieroglyphs around the room and ask students to decipher them, trying to discover whose name each might be. This is a fun activity for the class.

Carthage, Tunisia:
An Ancient Port

http://www.idsonline.com/tunisia/hist/hist.html
http://www.idsonline.com/tunisia/mosaics/mosaics.html
http://rome.classics.lsa.umich.edu/projects/lepti/lepti.html
http://www.rmwc.edu/Alumnae/carthage.html

Carthage, a jewel of ancient times, was an important trading center that now is occupied by the modern city of Tunis. Carthage's two excellent harbors afforded protection, harbored military ships, and served as a crossroads for commerce. Archaeologists believe that Carthage was founded around 814 BCE but have not been able to find remains later than 750 BCE.

On the Web site, students will travel along the northern coast of Africa where the hot winds blow across the Sahara and fan the beaches of the blue Mediterranean Sea. The Net site at Carthage brings to the novice and experienced archaeologist the text and photo history of the ancient site of Carthage, the people, their art, and their architecture. Beautiful photographs adorn this path to the past.

Lesson One: Relief Map of Ancient Carthage

Objective

The students will construct a replica of the peninsula, fortresses, and harbor at ancient Carthage.

Time Required

Two one-hour sessions

Materials

☐ Heavy cardboard (1-foot squares cut from appliance boxes, plus several strips measuring 12 inches long by 1 inch wide)

☐ Pencils

☐ Dough for each group or individual:
   2 cups flour
   ½ cup water
   1 cup salt

☐ Tempera paints

☐ Brushes

☐ Newspaper

☐ Plastic knife

Procedure

Following the discussion of Carthage and viewing of maps, students will build a relief map of this Mediterranean seaport labeling the points of interest and importance, for example, natural breakwater, fortresses, and sea walls.

Working in teams or individually, the students will draw in pencil the outline of Carthage on the cardboard provided. After mixing the flour and salt, they will make a dough, by slowly adding water until the dough is stiff and will hold a shape. Applying the dough with a plastic knife, strips of heavy cardboard, or fingers to the cardboard base (no licking fingers!), students will build the city harbor. After the dough dries, tempera paint can be applied to designate the sea, land, sea walls, ships, and so on.

Lesson Two: Where Is Carthage?

Objective

Students will participate in a mapping/geography exploration of North Africa.

Time Required

Thirty minutes in class
Independent work at home with parent

Materials

☐ Maps of Africa
☐ Colorful pushpins or stickers

Procedure

The teacher will review the objective of the lesson. Students will research the current countries of North Africa as well as ancient sites. Locate these places on the map. Use the tools of a map to discover the longitude and latitude of the site. Review the function of the key and compass rose. Plot position using brightly colored pushpins or stickers. Geographical characteristics such as mountains, rivers, plains, deserts, natural ports, and lakes can also be identified.

Students should provide a brief explanation of the discussed sites as well as a side note describing the people, time, and characteristics of the location. Include descriptions of both ancient and modern times.

This lesson can be expanded to varied levels of complexity depending on time and interest.

North America

Jackson's Hermitage, United States

Mesa Verde, United States

Jamestown, Virginia, United States

The Maya, Mexico and Central America

The Aztecs, Mexico

The Thule, Arctic North America

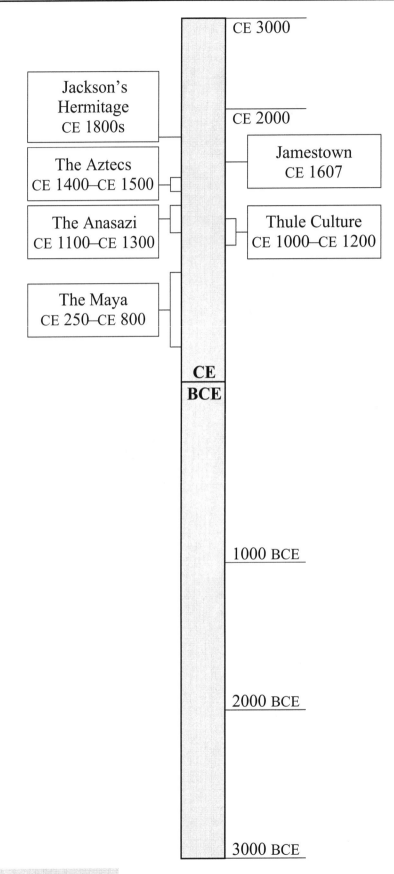

Timeline for North America

North America

North America is the third-largest continent in area. It extends from the Arctic in the north to South America in the south. The Atlantic Ocean is the eastern border and the Pacific Ocean spans the full length on the west. Indigenous peoples inhabited this land long before European explorers and conquerors set foot on the continent. Today, North America is rich in ethnic and geographical diversity.

1. Jackson's Hermitage, Tennessee, United States
2. The Anasazi, Mesa Verde, United States
3. Jamestown, Virginia, United States
4. The Maya, Guatemala and Belize
5. The Aztecs, Mexico
6. The Thule, Arctic North America

From *Dig That Site: Exploring Archaeology, History, and Civilization on the Internet.*
© 1997. Gary M. Garfield and Suzanne McDonough. Libraries Unlimited. (800) 237-6124.

Jackson's Hermitage, Tennessee, United States

http://www.earthwatch.org/x/Xmckee.html

Andrew Jackson's Hermitage, a plantation in Tennessee, flourished because of the labor of many slaves. During the excavation and ensuing research on this site, archaeologists determined the living conditions, cultural traditions, and diet of these slave laborers. Volunteers continue the work in an ongoing effort to piece together the life of the plantation slave in Tennessee in the 1800s.

Lesson One: An Exercise in the Concept of Freedom

Objective

Students will participate in a classroom experience relating to choice, decision making, rewards, and basic freedoms.

Time Required

Two hours

Materials

None

Procedure

Although no simulation, story, or account can truly bring the student to feel what life as a slave must have been like, we can promote a greater understanding of some of the underlying issues.

During one designated period, approximately one hour, teach your students the concept of equity by intentionally using strategies that are inequitable. The following are examples of what inequities you may establish:

1. Label half the class Group A and the other half Group B. Compensate Group A with snacks for completing classwork, participating in discussions, and helping in the classroom. Do not compensate Group B for the same accomplishments.

2. Students in Group A can sit in their chairs at the desks; Group B must stand on the side of the room. Group A students can move freely around the room; Group B students must raise their hands and receive permission before moving. Only a limited number of Group B students

will be permitted to leave their positions at any one time. Group A will have forty-five minutes for lunch; Group B will have only fifteen minutes for lunch.

3. Members of Group A will be praised and reinforced for classwork; the work of Group B members will be accepted *without* comment. Group A members will be looked at directly; the teacher will not directly acknowledge members in Group B. Group A members will be addressed by Mr. or Ms.; Group B members will be addressed by pointing. Group A members will be given points toward an end-of-the-week pizza party; Group B will be given no points.

After one hour, bring the students together and debrief them as to how they felt in these roles. How did Group A feel? How did members of Group B feel? Why? Would people choose to be in Group B? Why or why not? Expand the discussion, evaluating how this activity contributes to the class's awareness of some of the issues associated with slavery and freedom.

Lesson Two: The Life of a Slave

Objective

Following the reading of *The Slave Dancer* by Paula Fox, the students will compare living conditions on a slave ship with those faced on the plantation. Using evidence collected from the Internet as well as information in the novel, the students will reconstruct a picture of what life for the slave might have been like in the United States.

Time Required

Reading of the novel may take two to three weeks
Fifteen minutes per day for discussion

Materials

☐ *The Slave Dancer* by Paula Fox
☐ Writing materials
☐ Large piece of poster board or butcher paper
☐ Internet resources
☐ Library resources

Procedure

There are many novels that tell of the plight and hardships faced by the slaves during the early years of slavery. None leave as much of an impact on the reader as *The Slave Dancer* by Paula Fox. This Newbery Award–winning novel tells the story of thirteen-year-old Jessie and his plight after being seized from the dock of New Orleans. He is taken aboard a slave ship, where he is forced to play his fife as the slaves "dance" to keep their bodies fit for sale.

Each day, read a chapter from *The Slave Dancer* by Paula Fox aloud to the class. Following the reading, ask the students to record information on the following topics as they move through the chapters:

Living conditions

Diet

Punishment

Treatment of men, women, and children

Sickness and disease

The list can be put on poster board or a large piece of butcher paper so that the students can refer to it when doing their projects. Provide ample time for discussion on these most serious topics.

Instruct the students to create a project that reconstructs the life of a slave. Visit local libraries for social studies materials. Allow the students opportunities to search the Internet for Web pages that discuss the history of slavery in the United States. Encourage creativity in the presentations. Some students may choose traditional report formats; others may create their own Web site pages and multimedia presentations using commercial software.

The Anasazi, Mesa Verde, United States

http://www.mesaverde.org/mvnp/info/p1.html
http://www.worldmind.com/Wild/Parks/verde.html
http://www.jansport.com/kids/anasazi/anasazi.html
http://www.csulb.edu/gc/libarts/amindian/nae/chapter_1/001_002_1.07.jpg

Under the cliff outcropping at Mesa Verde, the Anasazi lived within a sanctuary of sandstone tribal villages tucked neatly and safely against nature's building blocks. These First Nation People were utilitarian architects and builders, diligently working to provide an organized, productive, and protected civilization. We will travel back to this time using the clues left behind. Reassembling the puzzle will tell us about the people, their daily lives, and the unique cliff dwellings. These sites will provide our young archaeologists a rich glimpse back to the years CE 1100 to CE 1300, when the Anasazi flourished. The visitor will view the cliff site today, the many artifacts from organized excavations, and, of course, the area as reconstructed by the many teams of social scientists who have devoted years to this precious cultural resource.

Lesson One: Cooking with the Anasazi

Objective

Students will participate in the preparation and consumption of a simulated typical Anasazi meal.

Time Required

Approximately one hour

Materials

- ☐ Electric skillet or small barbecue with charcoal and starter
- ☐ Several knives (not too sharp)
- ☐ Wooden spoons (no sterling in the cliff dwellings please)
- ☐ Yellow squash, corn on the cob with husks on
- ☐ Paper for covering the table
- ☐ Small paper plates for serving

Procedure

Ask your neighborhood produce store or produce manager in the supermarket for a donation. More often than not the response will be, "Of course, I will be happy to help." Be sure to send a thank-you note with a photograph of the event (suitable for framing).

The cooking can be done by one of your center groups. Use your normal organization for cooperative grouping. When cooking or using tools, *always* have an adult assisting/directing. Explain that you are going to make a "mash" from two of the typical foods of the Anasazi. First remove the husks from the sweet corn; set them aside. Pull away any remaining silk and discard. Holding the corn on end, use a knife to cut the kernels away from the cob. Be sure to demonstrate this and check for understanding. (A first aid kit is a desirable item in every classroom.) When the cutting is complete you will have a nice little pile of uncooked corn. Set aside.

Chop the small yellow squash into ¼-inch squares (triangles or rectangles are okay too). Mix the corn and squash together. Take the corn husks, overlap several, laying them flat on the paper-covered table. Put a small pile of the mixture in each of the husks. Fold the husks over and tie with strips cut from extra husks.

Lay the husks on a warm grill over low coals or cook slowly in the skillet. Turn several times, keeping the husks from burning. After about five to seven minutes, use the tongs to remove a sample and check for doneness. Distribute so that each student can taste the delicious treat. Discuss how this must have tasted after a long day's work. (You might mention that they also had squirrel, rabbit, and deer. And believe it or not, they raised turkeys!) Enjoy this special feast. Don't forget to turn off the skillet!

Whether your school is located on the side of a cliff or in the big city, you can add this firsthand knowledge to your understanding of the life and culture of the Anasazi.

Lesson Two: Anasazi Basket Making

Objective

The students will make baskets that incorporate the spiral twilled technique used by the Anasazi at Mesa Verde.

Time Required

One hour instruction time

Materials

Each student will need:

☐ One 24-inch piece of ¾-inch jute rope

☐ One skein four-ply yarn of any color or variation of colors

☐ Upholstery needle with a dull point and large eye

Procedure

The finest Anasazi baskets were woven using the spiral twilled technique. The baskets were used for carrying water, storing grain, and even cooking. Some baskets were lined with pitch to make them waterproof. When the Anasazi used baskets for cooking, they dropped heated stones into a basket that held water. The Anasazi wove their baskets using split willow, rabbitbrush, and skunk bush. Students will replicate the technique using material available today to create a decorative basket of their own.

A roll of jute rope can be purchased at your local craft store. Cut a 24-inch piece of ¾-inch jute for each student. This will be the coiled material that is used for the frame of the basket.

Each student will need a skein of four-ply yarn. You may ask students to bring in their own, appeal to parents who knit to donate old remnants, or ask a local yarn shop to make a donation of surplus materials. Students should be given the opportunity to choose the color or colors they would like to use, as the Anasazi baskets were handsomely decorated.

Cut a 15-inch piece of yarn and thread the upholstery needle. This length will keep the yarn manageable when wrapping it around the jute rope. If it is any longer, you will have tangles. Make sure the needle's eye is large enough so that the children will have no difficulty threading it themselves. If not, you will be an experienced needle-threader at the end of the activity and most likely will have become blind.

Step One: Creating the Base of the Basket

To start the basket, wrap the thread of yarn very tightly around the jute. When the first seven inches have been wrapped, coil the wrapped jute into a flat spiral or circle. With needle in hand, stitch the coiled piece together where it overlaps.

Step Two: Creating the Sides of the Basket

Continue wrapping the yarn and also coiling the jute to form the rest of the basket. To continue wrapping, count the number of yarn wraps you make around the jute. Wrap the jute five times with the yarn. On the sixth wrap, insert the needle under the coil below the one you are working on. Pull tightly. Again return to the single piece of jute and wrap it five times with the yarn. Once again on the sixth wrap, take the needle to the coil below, catch it with the yarn, pull tightly, and continue to wrap the single jute strand. When adding yarn, just cut a piece, thread the needle, and continue the procedure. Loose ends can be tucked in when the basket is completed. (Be sure to leave loose ends about 1/2 inch long so they will tuck in nicely.) Repeat this process until the jute is covered and the basket is completed.

The basket may take many days or weeks to complete. When not working on the basket, have students secure the needle in the yarn to keep it from unraveling. You may want to provide a designated time each day in class to work on the activity or instruct the students to work on their baskets as a quiet activity when they have finished other class work. You can also assign this project as homework. Just tell them that they can do this assignment while sitting in front of the television. They will give you a double look, smile, and think, "Wow, what a cool teacher!"

Jamestown, Virginia, United States

http://www.widomaker.com/~apva/

Jamestown was the earliest permanent English settlement in North America (not the earliest settlement by any means). In 1607 the tall ships *Godspeed, Discovery,* and *Susan Constant* carried over 100 settlers up the James River. The settlers quickly found their spot on a small island that later proved unsuitable for homesteading. Fire, drought, Indian attacks, and disease brought continued hardships on the settlers. The Indians and the settlers eventually formed alliances that brought temporary peace to the area. Visit the APVA Jamestown Rediscovery archaeology sites to be a part of this early North American village.

Lesson One: Agriculture in Jamestown

Objective

Students will participate in growing several agricultural products that may have been planted and consumed during the early years of the Jamestown settlement.

Time Required

Several hours over a two-day period
Maintenance time of a few minutes per day for the growing period

Materials

- ☐ Vegetable/fruit seeds of choice
- ☐ Gardening tools
- ☐ Stakes and string
- ☐ Fertilizer and mulch

Procedures

During the early years of Jamestown, the settlers at first resisted work; then resignation and the need to survive prompted the production of food to feed the inhabitants. This activity will foster student understanding of how long it takes to plant and harvest a crop.

First, visit a local nursery to determine a suitable crop for your climate. You can also go to the World Wide Web and check there. If you live in the West, check out *Sunset Magazine* for information related to growing vegetables in your zone. Once you have determined what you are going to grow based on climate, planting time, and harvest time, purchase or ask for donations of seed and mulch. Assemble the appropriate tools: shovels, hoes, rakes, trowels, string, and a few wooden stakes.

Walk around the school grounds and survey what might prove to be a good site for planting. Good daylight sun, accessibility to water, and safety from stampeding children going to and from recess are issues to consider. Mark off the garden site with rocks and a legible sign. You may need permission from the principal, but once you explain your project, you should have no problem. If you do, call us and we'll talk politics! You are ready to begin your Jamestown garden.

Divide your class into groups, with each group responsible for a portion of the garden. As a group, till the entire garden, preparing it for planting. The weeds and other plant matter should be gone, and the earth should look welcoming to our young farmers. Use the string to stretch between the wooden stakes to identify the rows. Use the hoes and shovels to dig the rows that will be used for irrigation and planting. If you are not using rows, forget the string and simply measure off basins several feet apart. It's an easier way to go and saves water.

Following the instructions on the seed packets, plant your seeds, water, eliminate weeds, and fertilize regularly. Watch your plants grow. Send teams out at intervals to chart and graph progress. When harvest time comes, plan a major feast like one that may have been prepared in Jamestown.

Lesson Two: A Letter Home

Objective

Students will write a letter to a dear friend in England describing the hardships they are facing in Jamestown. In the letter they should make comparisons between the harsh life in Jamestown and the life in England.

Time Required

One hour

Materials

- ☐ Paper
- ☐ Pencils
- ☐ Reference resources
- ☐ Internet resources

Procedures

Life at Jamestown was far more difficult than the settlers anticipated. First, they resisted the required work, and then they became victims of the hardships, many of which they created. Through class discussion, review the circumstances that brought the settlers from England to Jamestown.

Review the letter-writing format of the period. Samples can be found in traditional resource books or on the Internet. Instruct students to write a letter to a dear friend in England, describing the life and hardships faced in Jamestown.

Include in the letter the rationale for selecting the site, its discovered unsuitability, illness, conflicts, death, and despair. The teacher might also encourage the students to reflect upon what might be done to change their plight. Following applicable discussion and research, allot one hour for the students to complete the letters. Rewrites can be scheduled as needed.

The teacher will circulate and monitor student work, assisting with resources as necessary. At the conclusion, or following the rewrite, students may wish to share their letters or display them for others to read.

The Maya, Mexico and Central America

http://www.netaxs.com/~bampolsk/maya.html

The Maya were Native American people who developed and flourished within a magnificent civilization from about CE 250 for the next 600 years in what is today southern Mexico and Central America. The Mayan civilization was extremely advanced in writing, architecture, art, mathematics, and astronomy. The mystery of the Maya continues to be unraveled as further archaeological explorations and discoveries are made.

Uncover the mysteries of this ancient civilization as you journey through the maze of Mayan sites. Visit the Mayan Epigraphic Database Project to view hieroglyph graphics. Learn about Mayan history, mathematics, astronomy, language, and science. View pictures and maps of ancient ruins and become part of Mayan history as we explore a special people and culture.

Lesson One: Mayan Hetzmek Ceremonial Bag

The Mayan Hetzmek ceremonial bag was most often given to a child as a rite of birth. Within this sacred bag were placed items that were believed to guide the child through life. The Mayan people gave great importance to the many items that were chosen for inclusion.

Objective

The students will listen to the story *Rain Player* by David Wisniewski. In this beautifully illustrated story, they will discover ceremonial traditions of the Mayan culture, specifically the importance of the Hetzmek ceremony. This is described in the story and mentioned in the author's notes at the end of the book. The students will create their own Hetzmek ceremonial bag.

Time Required

One hour

Materials

- ☐ *Rain Player* by David Wisniewski
- ☐ Small brown paper bags
- ☐ Precut 10-inch strips of twine
- ☐ Items of importance to be placed in the bags, for example, charms (such as feathers, stones, shells, dried beans, corn, or marbles); family photographs; a favorite book; or a letter from a parent or friend. Students should collect their items of importance before beginning this activity and should secure permission from parents before bringing items from home.

☐ Crayons

☐ Markers

☐ Paint

☐ Paintbrushes

Procedure

Read *Rain Player* aloud to the class. Discuss the importance of the Hetzmek ceremony within the Mayan culture.

Distribute the small paper bags and twine to each student. Instruct the students to decorate their bags using the hieroglyph designs that are seen in the illustrations in the *Rain Player*. Use crayons, markers, and paints.

When the bag has been decorated, instruct the children to choose three or four items that have special meaning in their lives for inclusion in the bag. They can be the artifacts the children have brought from home, such as family photographs, a favorite storybook, a letter from a parent or friend, or a special charm.

Once the objects have been placed in the bag, the twine can be used to tightly close the opening. Ask the students to share why they selected the things they did and why they are important to them. Display the completed bags in a prominent place in the classroom for all to enjoy.

Lesson Two: Mayan Mathematics

Ancient ruins of the Mayan people provide evidence of a civilization advanced in mathematics. Cryptographers have determined that the Mayan numerical system is "vigesimal," using a base number of 20. Numbers are represented by a system of bars and dots; the dots are symbols for units of 1 and the bars, units of 5. Numbers are written vertically from bottom to top.

Objective

The students will identify and write numbers using the Mayan numeric system.

Time Required

One hour

Materials

☐ Numerical overhead transparency (fig. 4)

☐ Pencils

☐ Paper

Procedure

Make an overhead transparency or recreate the numbers on a large wall chart using the blackline provided. Explain to the students the vigesimal number system used by the Mayan civilization. Demonstrate that dots and bars represent units of value. Remind

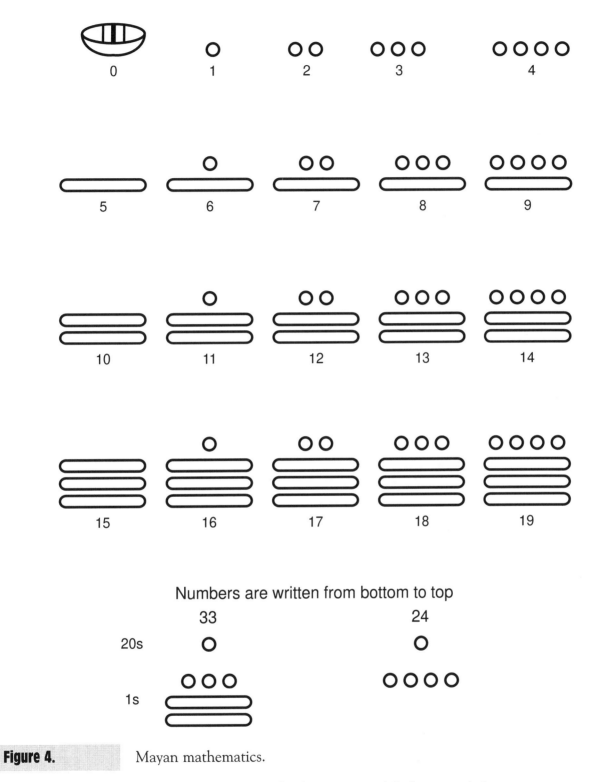

Numbers are written from bottom to top

the students that our base-ten number system uses place value to assign large values to digits. Show how place value is written in this ancient system. Demonstrate how we write our numbers horizontally and how the Mayans wrote vertically from top to bottom. Check for understanding as you proceed. Present the following questions to the students. Ask them to write the answer using the Mayan format:

> How many people live with you?
>
> How many children are in your classroom?
>
> How old are you?
>
> How many brothers and/or sisters do you have?
>
> How many people in the class have brown eyes?
>
> How many feet are wearing shoes with black shoelaces?
>
> How many students are wearing a watch?
>
> How many students are wearing earrings?

As a follow-up or independent activity, discuss the role numbers play in our society today. Identify their uses. Assign one of the following as an enrichment activity:

1. Create an address plate for your home using Mayan numbers.

2. Make a large poster displaying the classroom number. Decorate it using other Mayan hieroglyphs, which can be found on the Internet.

3. Collect the phone numbers of members of the classroom and create a telephone book.

The Aztecs, Mexico

http://kira.pomona.claremont.edu/mesoamerica.html
http://www.diva.nl/~voorburg/aztec.html
http://www.mexico-virtual.com/~nagual/calendar/

The Aztec civilization, which prospered during the 1400s and early 1500s in what is now southern Mexico, was one of the most advanced in the world. The Aztecs had large commercial centers, skilled artisans, a distinct language, and a complex religion. The Aztec empire was destroyed by Spanish conquerors, but their culture has had a lasting impression on those who followed. Archaeologists continue their work today, discovering new information related to this exciting American civilization.

The Aztec sites on the Net will guide the explorer to this awe-inspiring civilization. Learn about the language, art, climate, history, and social structure of these amazing and sophisticated people. See depictions of human sacrifices on the alters of the pyramids, and study the Aztec calendar stone, which represents the Aztec universe.

Lesson One: The Aztec Calendar

Objective

The students will make a replica of the famous Aztec sunstone, or calendar stone, also known as the stone of Axayacatl. Using the Internet pages provided, the students will discover what the various symbols represent and how the calendar was used in ancient times. Also using information found on the Internet, the students will translate Gregorian and Julian dates into Aztec dates.

Time Required

Three one-hour sessions

Materials

- ☐ Internet resources or traditional resources
- ☐ Construction paper of various bright colors
- ☐ Template of a 14-inch circle
- ☐ Rulers
- ☐ Protractors
- ☐ Glue
- ☐ Scissors

Procedure

Provide the students with the image of an Aztec calendar stone. You can either download the image from the URLs provided or find an example in a traditional resource found in most school libraries.

The original stone was carved in 1479 and was dedicated to the sun, the principal Aztec deity. The circular stone weighs almost 25 tons and has a diameter of less than 12 feet. The face of Tonatiuh, the sun god, is the center of the stone. Carved images are arranged in concentric rings.

Instruct the students to recreate the Aztec calendar stone using construction paper. Trace a 14-inch circle onto a piece of construction paper. This will serve as the base for the calendar. Be sure to use rulers and protractors to create accurate symmetry. Starting with the central disk, make the face of the sun god. Working away from the center, reproduce the rings and images that symbolize the Aztec universe. Cut triangles, circles, and rectangles to represent different parts of the stone. Glue these to the calendar.

After the calendars are completed, organize students into cooperative groups and access the Internet. The listed URLs provide images of the sunstones as well as the capability to click on any part of the graphic for a detailed description. As the students explore the site, they will discover the high level of technology and religious organization found in the Aztec culture. They can use the information to translate the Gregorian and Julian dates into Aztec dates. Follow the instructions provided on the Web site.

For the bold and daring teacher who has extensive bulletin board space, the class can recreate a full-sized calendar using the 12-foot diameter. Assign cooperative groups to create each ring. This would be a truly inspiring project.

Lesson Two: Lost to the Forest

Objective

The students will provide a demonstration of nature's method of reclaiming "disturbances" to the natural environment. Following the construction of a model temple within a flora environment, students will understand that if unattended, in time it will be reclaimed by nature.

Time Required

Constructing the model temple: One hour plus drying time
Establishing the miniplant environment around the structure: One hour
Observing the microenvironment: Several weeks

Materials

☐ Clay for temple construction

☐ Large jar with lid, a terrarium, a covered aquarium, or a covered fish bowl

☐ Variety of seeds and cuttings of small plants (ivy and other thick crawling plants to simulate the jungle or rain forest)

☐ Potting soil

Procedures

When the early archaeological field teams were searching for remnants of the Aztec civilization, the expeditions were hindered by the fact that the Spanish conquerors had decimated most of the temples and buildings, and the lush vegetation in the lowlands had reclaimed other structures that eluded both looters and scientists. This activity will demonstrate how the artifacts from our ancestors can quickly be camouflaged by the forest.

Have students construct a clay minitemple that will fit within the chosen glass container. The temple should probably be no more than a few inches in height. Let dry several days or until the clay is hard.

Lay moist potting soil evenly in the glass container, providing the largest horizontal surface. Position the hardened clay temple on the soil and plant seeds and cuttings. Be sure the environment is moist. Close the container and place in a bright environment but not in the direct sun (or the little plants will burn).

Observe the plant growth. Document through drawings or descriptive writing the process of forest reclamation. Hope you find your way out of the forest!

The Thule, Arctic North America

http://arts.uwaterloo.ca/ANTHRO/rwpark/ArcticArchStuff/ArcticIntro.htm

Brrr! Without question, the Arctic expanse in North America, stretching from Point Barrow to the west and Greenland to the east, reveals some of the most fascinating human adaptations found anywhere on the planet. The variety of discovered artifacts reveals movement of people over long distances and severe living conditions and provides a glimpse into the Thule culture of CE 1100 to CE 1200. The field scientist working in this harsh land also faces special challenges: short seasons for study, complex transportation and logistical problems, excavations into permanently frozen ground, and, certainly, the vastness of the area. Bundle up and join the High Arctic Canadian team members as they explore the early cultures of this extreme environmental arena.

Lesson One: Polar Bear Carving

Tiny bear carvings were relatively common finds from this period. Polar bears were the most often represented animal of these notable carvings. Our young archaeologists will recreate their carvings with Ivory soap instead of ivory from the tusks of endangered species.

Objective

Students will design and construct original bear carvings similar to those discovered in the northern Arctic expeditions.

Time Required

Forty-five minutes

Materials

- ☐ Ivory soap (one bar per student)
- ☐ Plastic knives
- ☐ Butcher paper (to cover desks)
- ☐ Photographs of bear carvings

Procedure

Following a study and discussion of the bear carvings most commonly found in the northern Arctic, students will be given the task of creating their own original carving. (This may be an appropriate time to discuss the use of ivory and why it is now illegal in many parts of the world to kill animals for their ivory tusks.)

After sharing some of the photographs of the miniature carved bears, the teacher should demonstrate carving techniques using the plastic knife and the bar of Ivory soap. Be sure to emphasize that each student will be given only one bar of soap; thus they should plan well and carve with care.

Following the allotted time, students may choose to share their carvings with the class. Proudly display them for all to see.

Lesson Two: Agriculture in the Arctic

Objective

The students will conduct an experiment comparing plants grown in an uncontrolled natural environment with plants grown in a controlled environment of harsh conditions.

Time Required

One hour for setup
Fifteen minutes per day

Materials

- ☐ Four plastic planting trays
- ☐ Potting soil
- ☐ Seeds
- ☐ Thermometers
- ☐ Access to a freezer on the school site

Procedure

The Arctic is a vast region of severely cold conditions. Plants usable for human consumption are limited. Winters are long and summers are short, preventing trees from growing larger than shrubs. Based on this information, the students will conduct an experiment to demonstrate the effects that cold temperatures and limited sunlight have on plants.

Pour potting soil into four plastic planting trays. Select a tray size that will enable you to place two into the freezer unit available on the school site. Make sure that you have informed the staff that this is going on. You would not want anyone to throw away the experiment (or eat it).

Ask your local nursery person to help pick out something that will grow quickly and that is not easy to kill. We want the children to experience success! Plant the seeds as directed on the package.

Two trays will be the control group. The plants in these will be grown as directed on the seed package. Select the appropriate spot for lighting, water as recommended, and talk to the plants if you like.

The remaining two trays will serve as the experimental group. Each day, after watering the plants, put the trays into a freezer for one hour. Assign a student to be the "keeper of the time." When the hour has passed, send two "runners" to retrieve the planters and place them in a dark location in the room. Tell the students not to go into the teacher's lounge unannounced.

Students can document the growth and changes of the plants by recording their findings as daily journal entries. They should document all observations including predictions, measurements, graphing results, and photographs.

Based on the results of their experiment, the students can discuss how the environment in a region affects the food supply.

South America

Tiwanaku, Bolivia

Caverna da Pedra Pintada, Brazil

Machu Picchu, Peru: The Lost City

Nazcan Lines: A View from Above Peru

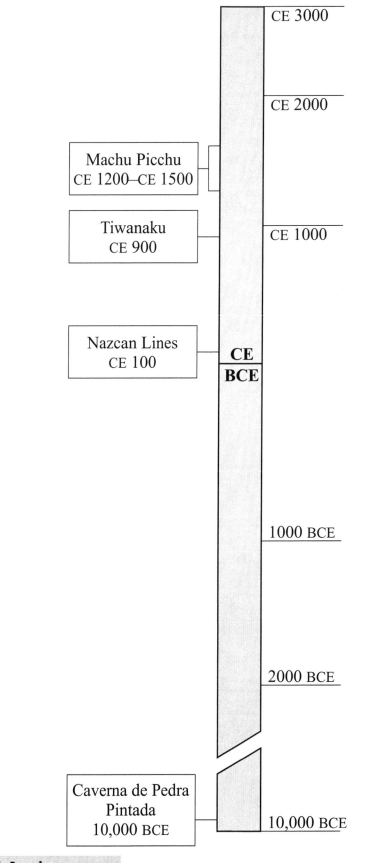

CE 3000

CE 2000

Machu Picchu
CE 1200–CE 1500

Tiwanaku
CE 900

CE 1000

Nazcan Lines
CE 100

CE
BCE

1000 BCE

2000 BCE

Caverna de Pedra
Pintada
10,000 BCE

10,000 BCE

Timeline for South America

From *Dig That Site: Exploring Archaeology, History, and Civilization on the Internet.*
© 1997. Gary M. Garfield and Suzanne McDonough. Libraries Unlimited. (800) 237-6124.

South America

South America has world-renowned rain forests, mighty jungle rivers, and majestic mountain peaks as well as one of the driest locales on the planet. Rich in natural resources and ancient history, it is a scientific treasure of artifacts for our young archaeologists. We will find the Lost City, visit farms in the swamps, explore dark caves, and unravel the graphic designs on the great plateaus.

1. Tiwanaku, Bolivia
2. Caverna da Pedra Pintada, Brazil
3. The Lost City of Machu Picchu, Peru
4. Nazcan Lines: A View from Above Peru

From *Dig That Site: Exploring Archaeology, History, and Civilization on the Internet.*
© 1997. Gary M. Garfield and Suzanne McDonough. Libraries Unlimited. (800) 237-6124.

Tiwanaku, Bolivia

http://larch-www.lcs.mit.edu:8001/~evs/bolivia/tiwanaku.html
http://www.farhorizon.com/bolivia/bolivia.html
http://larch-www.lcs.mit.edu:8001/~evs/bolivia/templo.html
http://larch-www.lcs.mit.edu:8001/~evs/bolivia/mapbol.html

A thousand years ago, the farmers of Tiwanaku in northern Bolivia cultivated the local swampland to feed a population that may have been between 40,000 and 120,000. These people created a terraced, renewable farm system out of what had been unproductive land. Archaeologists have recently shared these sophisticated techniques of raised-field farming with the current population, resulting in greatly increased production and a higher standard of living.

The visitor to the Net site will see walls, statues, canals, raised fields, stone-walled houses, and courtyards. Photographs, combined with the text, reveal an agricultural production system that may have been 400 percent more productive than systems used today.

Lesson One: Raising Veggies the Tiwanaku Way

Objective

Students will construct raised garden beds for vegetable production, as did the ancient farmers of Tiwanaku. Utilizing some of the same techniques of the ancient Tiwanaku, they will plant, maintain, and harvest vegetables.

Time Required

This project requires time for garden preparation and planting as well as maintenance time each week.

Materials

- ☐ Any of the following to be used as siding to hold raised beds:
  boards ½ to 1 inch thick and 10 to 12 inches wide

  large rocks (stacked to hold soil)

  slump stone or bricks (stacked to form walls to hold soil)

  railroad ties (lined end to end and stacked to hold soil)

- ☐ Soil, mulch, or a mix of both
- ☐ Seeds
- ☐ Watering hose
- ☐ Various gardening tools: rake, hoe, shovel, wheelbarrow

Procedure

After securing materials (of course, ask for donations from corporate sponsors, lumberyards, scrap yards, and home-improvement centers), build the walls of the garden. For boards, attach the siding at the corners with blocks of wood or corner braces. If using rocks, slump stone, or bricks, stack approximately 12 inches high. The area of the garden depends on material availability and space. Your garden can be a few square feet to an acre. Just remember, your class will have to maintain it. Fill the frames with soil, mulch, potting mix, or a mix of well-aged manure and local soil. Check with the local nursery to see what seeds will sprout in your climate. You can always use a gardening book from the local library or download information from the Internet.

Dig channels to serve as an irrigation system. Plant the seeds, water, and mark your crops. Maintain the garden, keeping it moist and weed free. Chart and graph your progress. Harvest your crops and have a class feast or donate the fresh produce to a local shelter or food bank.

Lesson Two: Synergy

Objective

The students will participate in an inquiry activity on the importance of synergy (groups working together).

Time Required

Three one-hour sessions

Materials

☐ Pencils

☐ Paper

☐ Traditional resources

☐ Internet resources

Procedure

The ancient people of Tiwanaku fed thousands by turning the local swamps into an innovative agricultural system. The concept was based on community participation to solve a problem that affected the entire population.

Instruct the students to solve the following problem (or design your own): In the soil surrounding ancient Tiwanaku, there are high levels of saline. Determine the impact saline has on agriculture. Resolve ways to eliminate the saline from the soil and reduce the amount found in the cultivated food items.

Divide the class into two groups. Group 1 will be the synergy cluster. These students will interact with one another to solve the problem. Encourage the students to call upon each other's knowledge and problem-solving skills to support the group's actions and decisions. Use the Internet to contact experts in the field. Utilize traditional resource material to gather information and statistics.

Group 2 will be made up of the remaining students in the class. These students will be required to work independently. They can use the same types of resources listed previously but all collected research information, skills, and expertise *must not be shared*. There is to be no communication among these individuals.

At the end of the allotted time period, bring the students together to orally present their solutions to the class. It is our experience that the group of students who have worked together will have developed a more complex and workable solution to the problem. This project demonstrates that a community effort is the most successful method for problem solving.

Caverna da Pedra Pintada, Brazil
(Amazon Cave)

http://www.bvis.uic.edu/museum/science/brazil.html

This archaeological find in the Amazon region of Brazil may change our understanding of the early peoples of this region and provide valuable information related to tropical forests and human evolution. This cave exploration, which has revealed stone spear points and remains of plants and animals, dates human life in the caves to some 11,000 years ago. The cave paintings might prove to be the oldest found in the Americas. They depict humans, animals, and composite creatures as well as geometric designs that may have astronomical significance. This site suggests that Paleoindians visited the cave regularly for 1,200 years and foraged for food in the rain forest and rivers.

Lesson One: Anatomy of a Cave

Objective

Students will create an "Anatomy of a Cave" collage.

Time Required

Forty-five minutes

Materials

- ☐ Black construction paper
- ☐ Drawing paper
- ☐ Scissors
- ☐ Crayons
- ☐ Glue sticks
- ☐ Magazines
- ☐ Internet or traditional resources

Procedure

Give each student a large piece of black construction paper. Instruct students to cut a shape that will represent an outline of a darkened cave. Students may choose to depict their caves in a variety of ways. Encourage different shapes and sizes.

Instruct the students to illustrate on separate pieces of drawing paper the objects, artifacts, and critters that might be found in one of the studied caves. They can cut out these individual drawings and glue them to the construction-paper cave. The students may also use magazines to find pictures of items that might be found in the caves.

Research the ecosystems within the dark caverns. Students can access the Internet or use traditional resources to find information. As items are placed on the cave, instruct the students to label each item.

On a large bulletin board, position the caves so that the passerby will stop to ponder what dangers and discoveries lay within the darkened caverns.

Lesson Two: Spelunking Class Video

Objective

Students will participate in a drama activity, producing a short video of cave exploration.

Time Required

Three forty-five-minute sessions

Materials

- ☐ Storyboard paper (paper with storyboard planning squares)
- ☐ Pencils
- ☐ Video camera
- ☐ Costumes

Procedure

Following the discussion of cave exploration, students will make a documentary (either serious or humorous) about spelunking.

Divide the students into groups of four. Students should design a storyboard outlining the scenes or frames for their video. One student per group should be instructed on the use of the video camera. Allow students with specialized talents to work in the areas that enhance their skills. Those with sewing skills can design and assemble costumes. Students with woodworking skills can design and construct the stages. As a language arts activity, the students can develop the script.

Select a site with appropriate lighting for the video production. This can be either indoors or outside. Shoot the video. Students can use various creative techniques such as turning the camera on its side or filming in unusual lighting conditions. This should be fun for all and quite possibly might earn the students an Academy Award!

Machu Picchu, Peru:
The Lost City

http://www.he.net./~mine/inca/plain.html
http://www.rcp.net.pe/promperu/TURISMO/machu-picchu-i.html

Machu Picchu was one of the great cities that served as home to the Inca, who inhabited this land from the 1200s to the mid-1500s until it was conquered by the Spanish. The Inca civilization flourished with master road builders, architects, and astronomers. The people were also dedicated warriors and lawmakers. On the Net you can walk among the ruins; view the city in the high clouds; see fountains, squares, streets, ancient huts, and stairways in the mist. Walk the Pyramid of the Sun and see the beauty of this once-walled Inca city.

Lesson One: Road Building Then and Now

Objective

Students will engage in research to discover the similarities and differences between road building during the period of the Inca and today.

Time Required

Two forty-minute sessions

Materials

- ☐ Internet resources
- ☐ Library resources
- ☐ Class history books
- ☐ Telephone

Procedure

Present the students with the following questions:

How were/are roads constructed?

Who was/is the labor force?

What equipment was/is used?

How were/are the paths for the roads surveyed?

Advise the students of all the resources available to them. Remind them that they need not be limited to just those listed here. Students can work either alone or in pairs. As they research and collect data, the students can formulate conclusions.

Bring the groups together to share and compare conclusions. Post the findings for all to see.

Lesson Two: Find Today's Lost City

Objective

Through research and problem solving, students will be able to identify the modern "lost city" through the clues provided by the teacher.

Time Required

Forty minutes

Materials

- ☐ List of clues provided by the teacher
- ☐ Paper and pencils to be used by student researchers

Procedure

Prior to the lesson, the teacher will select one or more cities in the world. Based on facts, geography and history, the teacher will write ten statements related to each place selected. These will serve as clues to the identity of the lost city. Each cooperative group will be given such a list.

When the "lost city" is tentatively identified, the students will check results with the teacher. The students will write a report that includes the clues, process, and conclusions as well as the resources used in the research process.

Nazcan Lines:
A View from High Above Peru

http://mud.aus.sig.net/ancnaz.html
http://kira.pomona.claremont.edu/nazca.html
http://indigo.stile.le.ac.uk/~rug/ar315/info/fotos17.html

Nazcan culture has provided modern humans with one of the great mysteries of all time: the Nazcan lines and massive figures constructed with white rocks in the desert. The Nazcan are also notable for their pottery, which is graceful, colorful, and different from that of other Peruvian cultures. The homeland of the Nazcan was within one of the deep gorges between northern Chile and southern Peru. The Nazcan inhabited this area some 1,500–2,000 years ago. Rain was rare, occurring only once every few years. This dry climate provided a perfect showcase for preserving archaeological finds.

Gigantic figures lined up in patterns that can be discerned only from the air have prompted some to speculate that they were put there by visiting aliens, perhaps to delineate runways for space vehicles. Others have theorized that they may be part of an ancient solar calendar. On this Web site, see the lines and figures as they appear from above. Is that a hummingbird carved in the land below? Who could have formed lines so geometrically perfect?

Lesson One: Learning from Great Heights

Objective

Students will discover that what can be seen from the air cannot always be seen from the ground.

Time Required

Forty-five minutes

Materials

Aerial photographs obtained from a local airport, air photography studio, downloaded from the Internet, department of transportation, or National Aeronautics and Space Administration (NASA). Attempt to obtain an aerial photograph of the local area. This will generate the most interest.

Procedure

Following a lesson on the Nazcan and what was observed from aerial photographs, share with the students an aerial photograph of a location they may be familiar with (one that has a large park, rivers, recreation, lake area, amusement park, schools and so on).

Divide students into cooperative groups. Distribute the local aerial photographs to the groups. Ask students to identify and list places or objects they are familiar with. Then have students note places or objects that they are unfamiliar with. They then can do a variety of research endeavors to discover what these views might be.

Lesson Two: Textile Dyeing

Objective

After viewing Nazcan textiles, the students will dye wool yarn using commercial dyes that produce natural colors.

Time Required

Two hours

Materials

- ☐ Five skeins untreated wool yarn, three- or four-ply
- ☐ Packages of dye (colors that represent natural hues, such as brown, blue, yellow)
- ☐ Large metal pot
- ☐ Wooden spoon

Procedure

Uncovered from the Nazcan archaeological sites are fine examples of tightly woven textiles. On these well-preserved samples are images of what appear to be hot air balloons. Archaeologists have surmised that the ancient Nazcans had the resources and the technology to create these airborne crafts. Thus, a thousand years ago, the lines may have been created to be viewed from the air.

Have the students recreate Nazcan textiles by first dyeing yarn. Dyeing in ancient times was done with natural dyes. However, natural dyes can be expensive, and the process is very time consuming. Commercial dyes are easy to use and less expensive.

Unravel the five skeins of wool yarn into large, loose loops. This will allow for equal absorption of the dye as the yarn sets in the dye vat.

To dye the yarn, follow the directions on the package. The procedure may vary depending on the commercial dye selected. Some require a heating process; others require only soaking in the solution. When making your selection, evaluate equipment available in your classroom and the amount of adult supervision required.

Once the yarn has been dyed, hang the skeins to dry overnight. When the skeins are completely dry, wrap them into balls. The yarn can be used for a variety of classroom projects. The students could weave colorful mats or braid the yarn into circular pads.

Australia
and the Pacific

Shipwrecks of Queensland

Aboriginal Stone Tools

Stone Giants of Easter Island

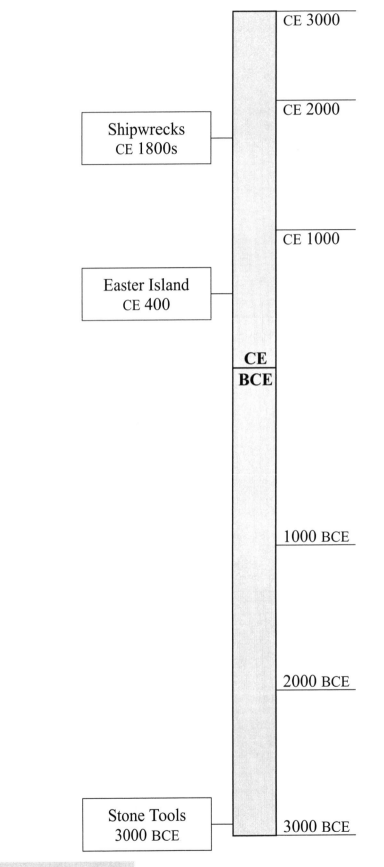

CE 3000

CE 2000

Shipwrecks
CE 1800s

CE 1000

Easter Island
CE 400

CE
BCE

1000 BCE

2000 BCE

Stone Tools
3000 BCE

3000 BCE

Timeline for Australia

From *Dig That Site: Exploring Archaeology, History, and Civilization on the Internet.*
© 1997. Gary M. Garfield and Suzanne McDonough. Libraries Unlimited. (800) 237-6124.

Australia

"Down under!" they say. That's because Australia, the only country on earth that is also a continent, lies entirely in the Southern Hemisphere. Australia is a land of great contrasts with arid barren interior deserts and modern seaside cities with great expanses of beautiful beaches. The population of Australia is mostly made up of descendants of the British and other European people; the Aborigines, who migrated from Asia several thousand years ago, are the indigenous people.

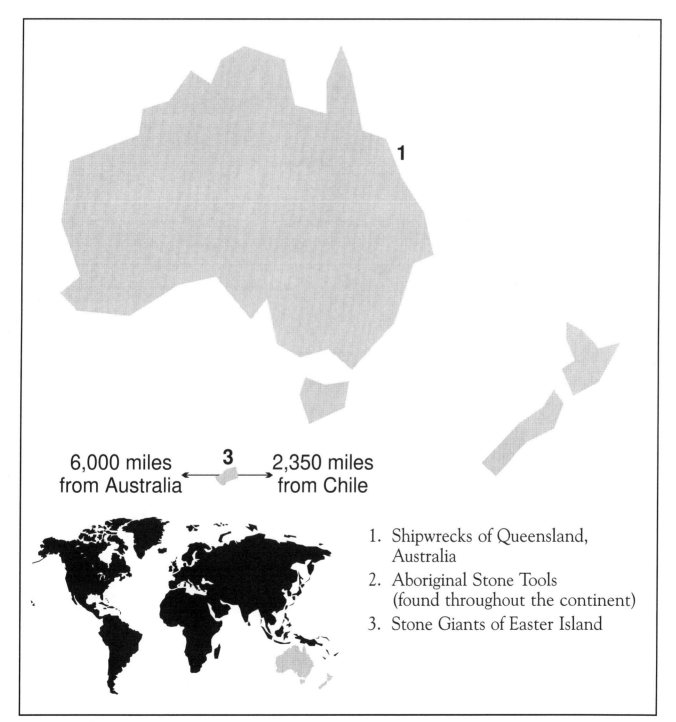

6,000 miles from Australia ← **3** → 2,350 miles from Chile

1. Shipwrecks of Queensland, Australia
2. Aboriginal Stone Tools (found throughout the continent)
3. Stone Giants of Easter Island

Shipwrecks of Queensland

http://www.mm.wa.gov.au/

For centuries, the explorers of the sea have ridden with or against the currents of the mighty oceans. Sometimes in peace, and sometimes in war, the vessels of humans have been used to reach the most remote places on the planet. From the days when Australia was the penal colony of the British Empire to the time when it was the "last frontier," the sea has been the highway to this country. For centuries, maritime vessels have met their fate on the many reefs of Australia. Some of these vessels were native to the continent; others were concluding months of journey as they crossed the oceans from Europe or North America.

Come to Queensland, Australia, where ocean vessels now rest in a quiet grave that you and other Net explorers can respectfully view. Simply click on one of the many shipwrecks off the coast of Queensland. See the maps, read the lists of shipwrecks, and learn about each ship, its crew, passengers, and purpose. View scores of photographs of these ghost vessels. This site exemplifies the science and art of maritime archaeology. Just like the sea, this site is always changing.

Lesson One: Life in the Great Barrier Reef

Objective

Students will draw a mural depicting past and present life-forms in the Great Barrier Reef.

Time Required

To be completed over a period of one week

Materials

- ☐ Butcher paper
- ☐ Pencils
- ☐ Crayons
- ☐ Tissue paper
- ☐ Construction paper
- ☐ Tempera paints
- ☐ Paintbrushes
- ☐ Glue
- ☐ Resource materials

Procedure

The reefs of the world have a special mystery; they are abundant with life of all forms. The Great Barrier Reef in Australia, extending over 1,250 miles, boasts 400 species of polyps and 1,500 species of fish and other animals including birds, turtles, crabs, and clams.

Our young maritime archaeologists will work in teams to create a decorative and detailed mural of the Great Barrier Reef. Designate groups to design specific aspects of the mural. Brainstorm. Pay special attention to the plant life, marine animals, and land features associated with this ecosystem. Be sure to include the documented shipwrecks and archaeological artifacts. Instruct students to recreate these in their mural.

To begin, students will sketch the design on a small piece of paper. When the members of the mural team are satisfied with the design, the image can be enlarged and transferred to the butcher paper.

Using twirled tissue paper, cut construction paper, tempera paint, glue, and whatever else is available in the supply room, begin the construction of the Barrier Reef. The mural can remain one-dimensional, or the students may choose to provide a three-dimensional twist by designing vegetation and animal life that "jump out" of the picture. Display in a prominent location for all to enjoy. Viewers won't have to wear those funny little blue and red glasses!

Lesson Two: Marine Archaeology Versus Underground Archaeology

Objective

The students will create a Venn diagram (see fig. 5) showing comparisons of marine archaeology to underground archaeology.

Time Required

Forty-five minutes

Materials

- ☐ Internet resources
- ☐ Archaeology research materials

Procedure

As the students begin to understand archaeology, have them explore the marine sites found in the Queensland area of Australia. Sunken deep beneath the water's surface, underwater sites present varied challenges for archaeologists.

Ask students to collect information pertaining to marine archaeology and underground archaeology from the many resources available to them. Generate lists that answer the following questions for each type:

How are sites located?

What tools and equipment are needed to excavate a site?

How do the elements affect the artifacts discovered?

What are the dangers or special challenges?

What are the daily routines of archaeologists at each kind of site?

Marine Archaeology Versus Underground Archaeology

Marine Archaeology   Underground Archaeology

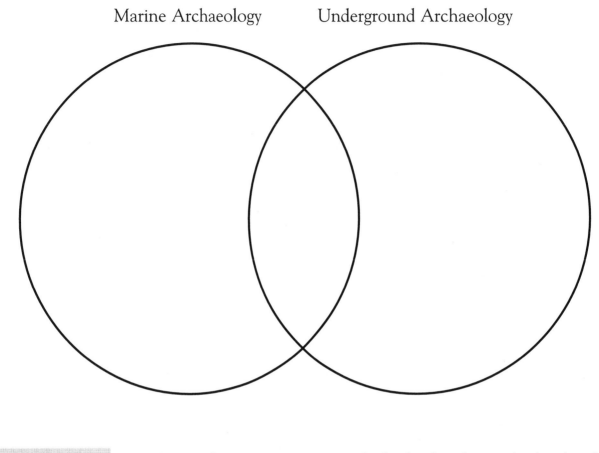

Figure 5.   Venn diagram for use in comparing methods of archaeology on land and under water.

From the information collected, create a Venn diagram showing the comparison of the topic areas. Draw two large circles on the board, overlapping them so that three sections are created. Label the section on the left "Marine Archaeology." Label the section on the right "Underground Archaeology." Put the information in the appropriate section of the diagram. Shared information can be entered in the section where the two circles overlap.

Aboriginal Stone Tools

http://www.ntu.edu.au/arc/arcrock.htm

The ongoing discovery of Aboriginal prehistoric stone tools all across the continent of Australia has aided in the mapping of early Australian Aboriginal history. It is interesting, for example, that these people of the Holocene era (10,000 years ago to the present), who lived some 5,000 years ago, did not carry their grinding stones with them as they moved from place to place with the seasons. Instead, they placed them upside down and left them in a memorable spot, to be used again upon their return. Visitors to the site will encounter pictures and text on some impressive collections of stone tools—blades, barbs, spears, hammers, axes. These tools were primarily used for stone- and woodworking, food preparation, hunting, ceremonies, and rituals. Click on photographs, a glossary, maps, and related sites.

Lesson One: Stones of Life

Objective

Each student will identify, select, and demonstrate the use of one stone that has characteristics of previously studied stone tools.

Time Required

Thirty minutes

Materials

- ☐ Rocks
- ☐ Strong plastic crate holding stones of varying shapes
- ☐ Heavy sticks that can be used for handles
- ☐ Brown twine that can be used to tie stones to handles
- ☐ Cardboard for backing cut 8 ½ by 11 inches (or as desired)
- ☐ Paper
- ☐ Pencils
- ☐ Glue sticks

Procedure

Collect rocks that are about the size of the students' fists. The teacher can visit a former riverbed or a rock quarry or may ask the students to bring them in from home.

Have the students select the stone of choice. In table groups, students can discuss the possible uses for their tool. Discuss the advantages of handles and why a tool might require one. Determine how the handle might be attached. Using twine, wrap the stone tightly to the stick. This can be difficult, so parent helpers are encouraged.

Once the students have finished the construction of their tools, they can share them with the class. Instruct them to write descriptions of how they were made and possible uses for their tools.

To display, glue the descriptions to the cardboard display backing. Lean the tools against the display board. This is a nice display for back-to-school night and open house.

Lesson Two: Stone Tools Used for Preparing Food

Objective

In order to recreate the methods for food preparation used by ancient Aboriginal tribes, the students will use grinding stones to crush seeds and nuts.

Time Required

One hour

Materials

- ☐ A variety of seeds and nuts: sunflower seeds, peanuts, acorns, pumpkin seeds
- ☐ Large grinding stones
- ☐ Smaller, handheld grinding stones

Procedure

Provide the students with stationary grinding stones. These should be large and flat. Most district resource centers have a stationary grinding stone for teachers to check out and use in the classroom. If this is not available, check with a local library or museum. Students can collect appropriately shaped smaller grinding stones from the surrounding area and bring them into class.

Place the seeds on the large, stationary stone. Using a smaller stone held tightly in the hands, begin to grind. Experiment with different types of nuts and seeds. Observe the differences in crushing husked nuts as opposed to those still in the shell. Determine if oil content affects the pulverizing process. Ask the students to predict the length of time it would take to mash a cup of any given type of nut or seed. From this calculation, the students can draw conclusions about the amount of time required to produce enough ground food for a small tribe.

Stone Giants of Easter Island

http://www.adventure.com/library/encyclopedia/ka/rfieaste.html
http://hea-www.harvard.edu/~adam/easterisland/ww.html
http://hawaii-shopping.com/~sammonet/rapanui.html

It may have been Native Americans or Polynesians who in CE 400 first inhabited these islands some 2,300 miles west of Chile. The islands were referred to as Rapa Nui, but the name of Easter Island came into use when in 1722, the Dutch admiral Jacob Roggeveen came across the forty-five-square-mile volcanic island on Easter Sunday. To the amazement of Admiral Roggeveen and others who were to follow, great 10- to 40-foot statues, some weighing up to 90 tons, dominated the beaches. No one knows how the great statues were moved and erected on the various sites of this small atoll. Following the Dutch occupation, the natives of the island suffered servitude, slavery, and death from mistreatment and disease.

Click on the shores of this small Pacific island and visit the relics of a mysterious, long-vanished civilization. All that remain are the extinct volcanoes and the scores of giant Godlike statues that peer out from the sloping shores across the sea. The photographs bring the wonders of this faraway place within the grasp of every young classroom archaeologist.

Lesson One: The Food of Paradise

Objective

Using tropical foods, students will assemble, cook, and eat a traditional vegetarian meal. (Yum, and so good for you!)

Time Required

One hour for preparation
Thirty minutes for cooking

Materials

- ☐ Knives
- ☐ Bananas
- ☐ Yams
- ☐ Brown sugar
- ☐ Banana leaves (ask your grocer or produce provider)
- ☐ Barbecue grill or hot coals in a small outdoor pit

Procedure

It is the fantasy of every island adventurer to pluck nature's bounties from the tropical plants and feast in the warm sunshine by the sea. Take your students on a very special culinary adventure.

Light the fire using all caution necessary within a school setting. As the coals are getting hot, assemble the ingredients. Lay the opened banana leaves side by side so that they overlap. If they are large leaves, cut them into pieces so that the total surface area is about 6 by 6 inches.

Cut the yams into slices. Place a few slices of yams and a slice of banana on the overlapped banana leaves. Sprinkle with brown sugar. Fold the banana leaves around the contents, being careful to tuck in the ends to form a small, neat envelope.

Place the packets on the barbecue grill or in the pit coals and cook over low heat, covered for thirty minutes or until yams are done. To serve, unwrap the leaves and eat the contents from their natural containers. Yummy!

Lesson Two: A Miniature Easter Island

Objective

The students will create miniature clay reproductions of the carvings found on Easter Island.

Time Required

One hour

Materials

- ☐ Internet resources or traditional resources
- ☐ Molding clay
- ☐ Wax paper
- ☐ Water

Procedure

Using the Internet or traditional resources, view the ruins of Easter Island. Discuss the enormity of the figures. Post photographs of Easter Island around the room so that the images can be referred to by the students.

Cover the worktable area with wax paper. This will not only prevent a mess on the table, but will allow the students to easily manipulate the clay.

Give each student a lump of molding clay. Instruct the students to create a figure similar to the ones viewed on Easter Island. Encourage the students to pound, push, pull, pinch, and squeeze (the clay, that is, not each other). As a reminder, point out the importance of creating a face that dominates the sculpture. When the students have finished their creations, allow the art to dry. Consult the directions on the package for specific information.

Display the objects in a prominent location in the classroom. Have the students align the figures in groups of four or five, modeling their presentation after the original site at Easter Island.

Antarctica

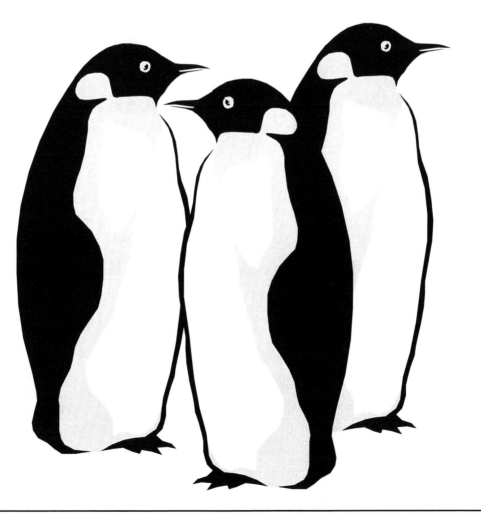

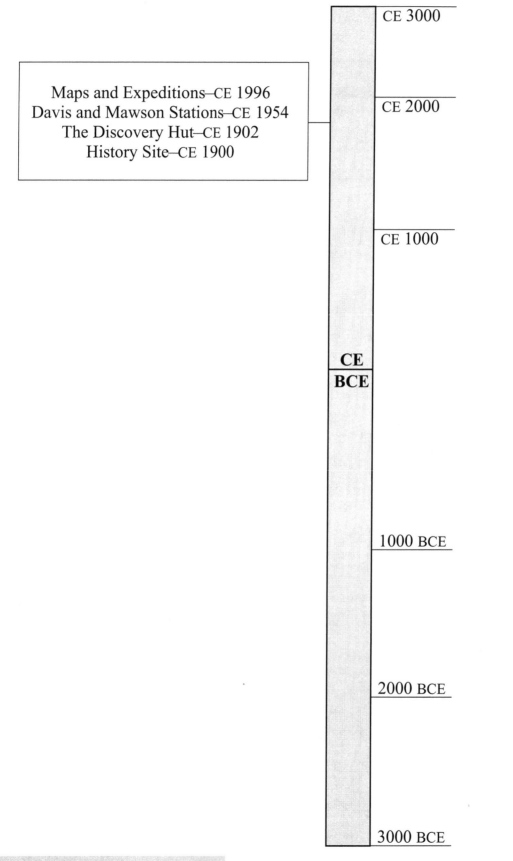

Maps and Expeditions–CE 1996
Davis and Mawson Stations–CE 1954
The Discovery Hut–CE 1902
History Site–CE 1900

CE 3000

CE 2000

CE 1000

CE
BCE

1000 BCE

2000 BCE

3000 BCE

Timeline for Antarctica

From *Dig That Site: Exploring Archaeology, History, and Civilization on the Internet.*
© 1997. Gary M. Garfield and Suzanne McDonough. Libraries Unlimited. (800) 237-6124.

Antarctica

Archaeologists search everywhere for remnants of past civilizations, even the frozen continent of Antarctica. Antarctica is the fifth-largest continent and is buried under a cap of about 7 million cubic miles of ice. The ice in some places is as much as 14,000 feet thick and reaches temperatures to minus 127 degrees Fahrenheit, the coldest recorded temperature on earth. Thus both habitation and archaeological expeditions have been limited on this continent.

1. The History Site
2. The Davis and Mawson Stations
3. The Discovery Hut
4. Expedition Map of Antarctica

The History Site

http://www.terraquest.com/va/history/chronology/chronology.html
http://www.terraquest.com/va/history/history.html

The Greeks, who argued that the planet was a sphere, believed that Antarctica served as a "balance" for the northern world. The discovery and exploration of Antarctica is very recent in terms of human history. This site depicts a starting point for the archaeologist who has an interest in piecing together exploration of this southern land. You will find a chronology of dis-coveries and expeditions as well as pictures, places, and names that may lead you deeper via the expanding links. Keep looking, keep searching, keep digging, and you will discover much of what was described as Terra Australis Incognita, or The Unknown Southern Land.

Lesson One: A Walk Back in Time

Objective

Students will construct a timeline of the people and the artifacts during the exploration of Antarctica.

Time Required

Several forty-minute periods over a week

Materials

- ☐ Butcher paper, cork display board, or three-part science display board
- ☐ Miscellaneous materials for artifacts
- ☐ Markers
- ☐ Glue
- ☐ Colored construction paper
- ☐ Other materials as creatively identified

Procedures

This activity can be accomplished as one timeline for the entire class with each student taking one event or time period or as several timelines using cooperative groups. Following the study (teacher directed or independent student research) students will construct a timeline using whatever materials they wish. With each exploration event designated, students will either draw a picture depicting the event or construct a facsimile of an artifact that represents that event. These depictions and/or artifacts will be attached to the timeline and displayed for all to view.

The Davis and Mawson Stations

http://www.camtech.com.au/mawson/background.html
http://www.antdiv.gov.au/aad/exop/sfo/mawson/video.html
http://www.noao.edu/noao/staff/keller/anta95fig.html

Australia is among the many nations that have conducted scientific exploration in the Antarctic region. Located on the eastern side of Holme Bay on a horseshoe-shaped rock outcropping, the Mawson Station was established in 1954 and has the distinction of being the oldest continuously occupied station on the continent. The Davis station was established three years later. These explorers carried out their scientific investigations using the latest equipment of the time within an environment that is a challenge to the emotional and physical well-being of any inhabitant.

Those venturing into this frozen wilderness will see pictures from Mawson Station. Students can chart the weather, learn about the early explorers of this territory, and see magnificent vistas. View the old buildings or huts that housed these explorers. This area is being searched for evidence of the Norwegians Caroline Mikkelsen, the first woman to explore this region, and her husband, who in 1935 are believed to have built and lived in a primitive camp in the area. Site-seers can learn more about the exploration of this continent through the links that are becoming available. Dig in as we head south to search for clues in this very "cool" site.

Lesson One: Looking Back from the Year 2900

Objective

Students will collect data from the Antarctic discovery period of the early 1900s and make assumptions about the culture of the time.

Time Required

Three forty-minute sessions

Materials

- ☐ Internet resources
- ☐ Library resources
- ☐ Paper
- ☐ Pens

Procedure

Review with students the learning objective, of viewing and collecting data on the Antarctica discovery period from the perspective of people living in the future year 2900.

In cooperative groups, students will collect data on the expeditions and the living conditions. They will categorize the data, such as pictures, documents, stories, and journals, into groupings that make sense. Based on their research, the students will make assumptions about the culture that existed at the site and elsewhere during that time period. Students can share their assumptions with other groups, comparing and contrasting findings and conclusions.

The Discovery Hut

http://www.ssec.wisc.edu/~rbrbrn/discoveryhut.html
http://channel.isle.net/~teddyt/photos/Antarctic_landscape.jpg

The Discovery Hut was brought from Australia to the region by early settlers in 1902 and survives to this day. Sitting silent and remote, it overlooks Winter Quarters Bay, McMurdo, Observation Hill, Caper Armitage, McMurdo sound, and the Western Mountains. In this building that is thirty-six feet on each side, Robert Scott and his expedition dried furs, skinned birds, and rehearsed and performed plays and skits. Really! See the actual hut and provisions that still remain.

Lesson One: Designing and Equipping a Discovery Hut

Objective

Students will design a "hut" that will withstand the weather conditions of Antarctica, and will compile a list of essential staples needed for survival.

Time Required

One hour

Materials

- ☐ White drawing paper
- ☐ Pencils
- ☐ Markers
- ☐ Crayons

Procedure

Following the teaching or independent study on the early expeditions, provide students with general directions related to their task of designing a living/working hut and the items most necessary for survival.

Students will design and draw a hut that could withstand severe Arctic weather. They should include in their drawings the contents of the storage shelves and other provisions that would aid in the discovery party's survival. Share and display.

Lesson Two: Winter in July

Objective

Students will describe and illustrate the weather in Antarctica during the months of January and July.

Time Required

One hour

Materials

- ☐ Internet resources
- ☐ Physical geography books
- ☐ Information sheets related to the seasons, earth's axis, rotations, and so on
- ☐ Paper
- ☐ Pens
- ☐ Crayons

Procedure

Students will draw pictures of an expedition site, including the buildings and activities, for the months of July and January. Students will share and post the pictures with explanations.

Expedition Map of Antarctica

http://www.terraquest.com/va/expedition/maps/cont.map.html
http://psc.apl.washington.edu/ISWphotogallery/ISWphotogallery.html

For centuries kings, explorers, scientists, and visionaries have been making maps to chart their explorations, conquests, and dreams. The Greeks included a southern land mass, thought to be Antarctica, in their maps; they supposed this continent provided a balance to the Northern Hemisphere. The map in the first Net site listed here provides insights to the various expeditions that have sought answers to the mysteries of this most southern continent. It also includes national claims and points of interest. Students searching the map will be able to make conclusions about the explorers and their times.

Lesson One: Mapping Skills

Objective

Students will strengthen mapping skills by identifying specific locales on the map of Antarctica.

Time Required

Forty minutes

Materials

- ☐ Duplicated maps of Antarctica
- ☐ Demonstration map on the overhead projector
- ☐ Pens

Procedure

The teacher will provide direction for the task. Using landmarks, degrees, longitude, and latitude, students will "discover " and problem solve, attempting to locate places of interest or geographical significance on their personal maps.

1. Students can plan an overland exploration following the least treacherous route.

2. Students can plan an exploration of Antarctica traveling mostly by sea.

3. Students can identify what countries have claimed territory within Antarctica, as well as when and for what reasons, and can determine what exists in these locales today.

Lesson Two: E-mail Correspondence with an Antarctic Research Station

Objective

Students will identify an Antarctic scientific research project via the Internet and begin a learning dialogue with the scientists, contacting some of the current scientific stations by e-mail and asking questions.

Time Required

Fifteen minutes, twice a week

Materials

- ☐ Internet resources
- ☐ Maps
- ☐ Paper
- ☐ Pencils

Procedure

Designate cooperative groups within the classroom. Access the Internet and identify scientific sites for possible connection. Instruct the groups to determine what site(s) they will contact and why.

Design preliminary questions that are related to the topic of study. Initiate contact through e-mail, according to a teacher-designed schedule. Send e-mail and check the account regularly for responses. Engage in an ongoing dialogue. Print and post all outgoing and incoming messages. Maintain a journal of communications.

Appendix A
Personal Site Journal

This is the place where you add your own archaeological site discoveries. Note the site, the URL or address, and provide a brief description for future reference. It is likely that this page will quickly fill as you continue your expeditions.

Continent	Name of Site	URL/Address	Description or Notes

Continent	Name of Site	URL/Address	Description or Notes

Appendix B
Suggested Journals, Organizations, and Resources

Following is a partial list of journals, organizations, and other resources that may prove useful when integrating the Internet or other technology into your daily classroom curriculum. Don't hesitate to contact these resources.

America Online
8619 Westwood Center Drive
Vienna, VA 22182-2285

Authors' E-mail
gmgarfield@csupomona.edu
smcdono@cyberg8t.com

Classroom Prodigy
2364 Harcourt
San Diego, CA 92123

CUE Newsletter
Computer Using Educators, Inc.
1210 Marina Village Parkway, Suite 100
Alameda, CA 94501

Custom Computers for Kids
3 Oak Forest Road
Novato, CA 94949

Educational Leadership
Journal of the Association for Supervision
and Curriculum Development
1250 N. Pitt Street
Alexandria, VA 22314

Electronic Learning
Scholastic, Inc.
555 Broadway
New York, NY 10012

Kappan
Phi Delta Kappa
P.O. Box 789
Bloomington, IN 47402-9961

MacWAREHOUSE Catalog
P.O. Box 3013
1720 Oak Street
Lakewood, NJ 08701-3013
1-800-255-6227

Net Guide
P.O. Box 420355
Palm Coast, FL 32142-9371

Teaching K-8
40 Richards Avenue
Norwalk, CT 06854

Site Index

Anasazi, the
      http://www.mesaverde.org/mvnp/info/p1.html
      http://www.worldmind.com/Wild/Parks/verde.html
      http://www.jansport.com/kids/anasazi/anasazi.html
      http://www.csulb.edu/gc/libarts/amindian/nae/chapter_1/001_002_1.07.jpg

Antarctica
   Davis and Mawson stations
      http://www.camtech.com.au/mawson/background.html
      http://www.antdiv.gov.au/aad/exop/sfo/mawson/video.html
      http://www.noao.edu/noao/staff/keller/anta95fig.html
   Discovery Hut
      http://www.ssec.wisc.edu/~rbrbrn/discoveryhut.html
      http://channel.isle.net/~teddyt/photos/Antarctic_landscape.jpg
   expedition map
      http://www.terraquest.com/va/expedition/maps/cont.map.html
      http://psc.apl.washington.edu/ISWphotogallery/ISWphotogallery.html
   History Site
      http://www.terraquest.com/va/history/chronology/chronology.html
      http://www.terraquest.com/va/history/history.html

Arctic North America
   Thule, the
      http://arts.uwaterloo.ca/ANTHRO/rwpark/ArcticArchStuff/ArcticIntro.htm

Australia
   Aboriginal stone tools
      http://www.ntu.edu.au/arc/arcrock.htm
   shipwrecks of Queensland
      http://www.mm.wa.gov.au/

Authors' e-mail addresses
      gmgarfield@csupomona.edu
      smcdono@cyberg8t.com

Aztecs, the

> http://kira.pomona.claremont.edu/mesoamerica.html
>
> http://www.diva.nl/~voorburg/aztec.html
>
> http://www.mexico-virtual.com/~nagual/calendar/

Bolivia
> Tiwanaku

>> http://larch-www.lcs.mit.edu:8001/~evs/bolivia/tiwanaku.html
>>
>> http://www.farhorizon.com/bolivia/bolivia.html
>>
>> http://larch-www.lcs.mit.edu:8001/~evs/bolivia/templo.html
>>
>> http://larch-www.lcs.mit.edu:8001/~evs/bolivia/mapbol.html

Brazil
> Caverna da Pedra Pintada

>> http://www.bvis.uic.edu/museum/science/brazil.html

Central America. *See* Mexico and Central America

China
> tomb of Qin Shihuangdi

>> http://www.adventure.com/library/encyclopedia/ka/rfitcarm.html
>>
>> http://www.c.hiroshima-dit.ac.jp/cnetservice/10places/xian.html
>>
>> http://www.hansonlib.org/bmaxian.html

Cyprus
> Marki Alonia

>> http://www.latrobe.edu.au/www/archaeology/marki/

Dead Sea Scroll. *See* Israel

Easter Island

> http://www.adventure.com/library/encyclopedia/ka/rfieaste.html
>
> http://hea-www.harvard.edu/~adam/easterisland/ww.html
>
> http://hawaii-shopping.com/~sammonet/rapanui.html

Egypt
> pyramids

>> http://pharos.bu.edu/Egypt/Wonders/pyramid.html
>>
>> http://galaxy.cau.edu/tsmith/Gpyr.html
>>
>> http://199.182.229.110/Exhibits/ADAE/fig23d.htm
>>
>> http://pami.uwaterloo.ca/~reda/kings/kings.html
>>
>> http://www1.usa1.com/~madartis/EGYPT/EGYPT.html
>>
>> http://www1.usa1.com/~madartis/EGYPT/alphabet.html

pyramids of Giza

http://pharos.bu.edu/Egypt/Wonders/pyramid.html

http://galaxy.cau.edu/tsmith/Gpyr.html

http://199.182.229.110/Exhibits/ADAE/fig23d.htm

tomb of Tutankhamen

http://pami.uwaterloo.ca/~reda/kings/kings.html

http://www1.usa1.com/~madartis/EGYPT/EGYPT.html

http://www1.usa1.com/~madartis/EGYPT/alphabet.html

England

Stonehenge

http://www2.ucsc.edu/people/trillian/stonehenge/start.html

http://www.gold.net/users/iy12/aaes/astroarc.htm

http://avebury.arch.soton.ac.uk/LocalStuff/Stonehenge/stonehenge.html

France

Paleolithic-Era painted caves

http://mistral.culture.fr/culture/gvpda-en.htm

Greece

Athens

http://www.indiana.edu/~kglowack/Athens/Athens.html

Israel

Dead Sea Scrolls

http://sunsite.unc.edu/expo/deadsea.scrolls.exhibit/intro.html

http://world.std.com/~caesar/FILES/DS/facts.html

Masada

http://www.stelcom.com/inpa/masada.html

http://www.register.com/triumph/p12.htm

http://www.ior.com/~jmcmath/masada6.htm

http://www.ior.com/~jmcmath/masada2.htm

Italy

Pompeii

http://enterzone.berkeley.edu/ez/e2/articles/frankel/tourlist.html

http://www.theplumber.com/pom.html

http://jefferson.village.virginia.edu/pompeii/page-1.html

Jordan

Petra

http://www.activelife.com/jordan/

http://www.mit.edu:8001/activities/jordanians/jordan/petra.html

Index

About the Authors

Gary M. Garfield is a professor of education at California State Polytechnic University, Pomona. For 20 years his primary focus has been the preparation of new teachers. Recent efforts have been directed in the area of integrated social studies

curriculum with telecommunications for pre-service and in-service classroom teachers. His areas of university teaching include reading instruction, educational psychology, dynamics of teaching in a pluralistic society, general methodology, organization of schooling, clinical supervision, early field experience, and introduction to classrooms and schools. Garfield has presented at national, state, regional, and local professional conferences and workshops. He is an educational consultant for school districts within a variety of teaching areas. Garfield holds California teaching credentials in elementary and secondary education, special education, administrative services, and community college. He has earned a doctorate in educational management.

Suzanne McDonough is currently a technology mentor teacher and fourth-grade classroom teacher in the Mountain View School District, Ontario, California. She is a teacher of both primary and upper-grade students, with an emphasis on the thematic approach to elementary school teaching using telecommunications in the classroom. McDonough has been a presenter at national, state, and regional association conferences and county offices of education. She serves as an educational consultant committed to equal access to information for all learners.